HOUSTON'S MOST WANTED

How I lived a life of crime for
many years until my heart was changed.

LT SHAW

WestBow Press books may be ordered through booksellers or by contacting:

WestBow Press
A Division of Thomas Nelson & Zondervan
1663 Liberty Drive
Bloomington, IN 47403
www.westbowpress.com
844-714-3454

Scripture taken from the King James Version of the Bible.

ISBN: 978-1-6642-6085-6 (sc)
ISBN: 978-1-6642-6087-0 (hc)
ISBN: 978-1-6642-6086-3 (e)

Library of Congress Control Number: 2022904886

Print information available on the last page.

WestBow Press rev. date: 03/21/2022

To all those who are tired of running.

CONTENTS

Acknowledgments ix
Preface xi
Introduction xiii
Chapter 1 The Making of a Thief 1
Chapter 2 The Nissan Frontier Tank 10
Chapter 3 Through the Walls 23
Chapter 4 The Loaded Judge 35
Chapter 5 Escape to the Clearing 62
Chapter 6 The Golden Key 77
Chapter 7 Booby-Trapped Pawnshops 98
Chapter 8 I Was Shot! 111
Chapter 9 Escape by Four-Wheeler 119
Chapter 10 Robbing the Printshop 131
Chapter 11 Houses in the Millions 139
Chapter 12 My Penthouse Lair 149
Chapter 13 One Inch from Death 157
Chapter 14 Crawling through the Poop 163
Chapter 15 The Traveling Car Lot 168
Chapter 16 Arrest and Trial 173
Chapter 17 Surviving in Prison 183
Chapter 18 The Great Escape Mistake 196
Chapter 19 How One Touch Changed Me 204

Chapter 20 Halfway Home 218
Chapter 21 What Do I Do Now? 224
Appendix A: The Penthouse Lair 231
Appendix B: The Original *Galveston Sentinel* Houses 233
Appendix C: Map of the Location of the Houses 235
Appendix D: GPS Locations of the Gold 237
Appendix E: The Bucket with Gold Bars 239
Appendix F: The Judge's Watches 241
Appendix G: Notes on the *Galveston Sentinel* Houses 243
Notes 245
About the Author 247

ACKNOWLEDGMENTS

I would like to thank all the men who helped me on my path.

PREFACE

This book is based on truth, true lives, true stories, and true crimes. The names have been changed to protect the guilty.

I kept my name secret for several reasons. I am still alive, and the gangs or the law could still have something on my record I'm not aware of. Read the book as if *you* are in the driving seat. However, I hope you don't get carsick.

These are some of the characters in this book:

Hank, my mentor

Janet, my sweet wife and partner, who I miss

Amanda, my ex, who I don't miss her

Simon, my brother.

Alberto Espinoza, the gang lieutenant I saved from assassination

Fred, my nephew and mentee, who was convicted for federal crimes

Bubba, who helped me rob a parts store

***

While you were asleep, I robbed you blind, Houston. I stole from your prints hops, your parcel delivery businesses, your pawnshops. I stole your cars with your own keys, and I enjoyed the lifestyle of a millionaire without ever working.

I was caught a few times, spent several Christmases in prisons, but had a stash of gold buried at Galveston Island, and as soon as they released me, I had the capital to rapidly start up my devious enterprise.

This is my story, as it really happened; the names have been changed to protect the guilty.

I was *not* a violent criminal. If you are looking for violence, find yourself another book. My forte was taking what was not mine and running with it. I never committed acts of violence, but I did break the eighth commandment, "Thou shalt not steal," a lot.

I was always running and always tired of running, often kept just one step ahead of the Houston PD, but their persistency did pay off.

I was Houston's Most Wanted, and this is my story. This is how I got my name on the Houston Most Wanted list—by robbing Houstonians mostly and running from the law for many years.

INTRODUCTION

I was born on Galveston Island, on the southeast side of Texas, about an hour's drive from Houston, Texas. Galveston is a quaint island, about 27miles long and no more than 2miles wide at its widest point. Galveston is almost twice as long as Manhattan Island but just a little bit wider. (Manhattan is 13.4 miles long and 2.3 miles wide.)

The street numbering is similar to that in Manhattan. As you reach the residential area, right past Ferry Road, it starts with 1st Street. And it ends with 103rd Street.

The streets run the length of the island; the avenues cross them and cut the island into neatly organized rectangular blocks. The avenues go from "A" to "U," with some halves in there, like Avenue Q1/2 Rear and so on.

Most people don't venture far from the beach and the hotel they stay at or the trendy Strand area. Lately, with the arrival and departure of cruise ships on the opposite side of the island, some people have ventured into the residential neighborhoods.

That's where I was born. My parents lived on Driftwood Lane; if that had anything to do with me becoming a "driftwood," I don't know.

My father was a pastor of the Saint Paul's Lutheran Church on Ave O for many years. My dad was a very kind man, not prone to discipline, but my mom made up for it. I got more spankings than my brother and sisters combined, and I deserved every one of them.

My dad was supposed to have been relocated every four years, to another congregation, but he refused to leave. He told the synod, these are my sheep. I will not leave them. I will shepherd them. Not only was that good for him and the congregation, but it was especially advantageous for me.

I was able to roam all over the island, mostly on my bicycle. To the east of our house was the older residential area, mostly wooden houses. To the north of us was the bayou, I could see the water from my bedroom window. To the west of our home was an industrial area, where they later built Bountiful Gardens and the pyramids. But when I was young, I would walk that beach for hours and walk back through the swamp of the Sydnor Bayou, circling the airport and making my way home slowly, very slowly.

My mom never worried about me. She knew I was fast and sly and could outwit anybody, including adults with evil intent. She and my dad made a trip to Switzerland before we were born, and she brought back a cowbell. This bell was five inches tall, three inches wide, and very loud.

If she knew we were outside playing and possibly in the industrial area or roaming the shore, she would go to the top floor of the house and ring that bell. We knew that meant: "Come home immediately for supper, or any other reason, and avoid the wrath of Mom and a whooping!"

We always made a beeline for the house when we heard that bell.

Some days, I would ride my bike all the way from 57thStreet to 8thStreet and back. I would tell my mom first that I would be riding to the tip. She told me to stay between Broadway and the seawall and to be back for supper. My bike had a big basket on the back and a small basket on the steering wheel. Often, I would find things people left on the side of the road or things they lost.

One time, I took something, a wallet, that was lying on top of a car. I should have left it there, but I swiped it. It had almost $500 in there. I took the money out and threw the wallet in the bushes. That was my first theft. I was fifteen years old. My conscience bothered me for a long time. I never told my mom or my siblings. But they often wondered how I could always be eating ice cream, while mom had nothing in the freezer that day.

Perhaps it was borderline finding/stealing in my mind, but it was the beginning of easy money. If I had to mow a yard in the hot sun for two hours for $10, or I could swipe a wallet in one minute for $500, the math was easy.

My dad would inevitably preach on the eighth commandment that Sunday, and we had to be in church in our white shirts, lined up next to my mom. Did my dad know? I knew God knew, but I put that as far away in the back of my mind as I could.

My dad passed away when I was in my twenties. My mom moved into a smaller house and later into assisted living.

I met Hank in Galveston. Hank was different. He always seemed to have money, but I never saw him work. He took me under his wing. My mentor, my first mentor, he led me along a wide road. My last mentor, many years later, would be a better one, but that's for the end of the book.

CHAPTER 1

THE MAKING OF A THIEF

A child is born in innocence. He or she might be naughty and disobedient, as I was, but stealing as a lifestyle has to be learned. I learned from Hank. I mentioned him in the introduction.

As I mentioned before, I was raised on Galveston Island, where Jean Lafitte buried his treasure. I buried mine there also.

As a preteen, I was allowed to roam pretty much the whole island on my bicycle, as long as I didn't get in trouble and was home for supper.

A few blocks from our house lived a man called Hank. His house was large. He had a four-car garage and always had four cars. Two of them were always the same—a Toyota Land Cruiser and a Saab. The other two cars seemed to be always different. Much later, I learned that Hank traded with the traveling car lot and that those cars were stolen. That was why he always kept those garage doors locked. And even in the garage, he kept them covered with a tarp.

Those were the cars Hank used to "organize" stuff—the euphemism for stealing. The cars were untraceable and could be dumped anywhere. A practice I employed often during my career was to always have one or two vehicles parked at my apartments.

Hank was usually at home. As a teenager with nothing to do during the summer, I did odd jobs for him. He was usually evasive when I asked what work he did. And since he always seemed to have money and was an easygoing guy, I didn't ask him any more questions.

Even though there was a forty-year age difference between us, we hit it off from the start. We became good friends. My parents met him once. They liked him too, and they didn't mind me hanging out with him. If they'd only known what path Hank's mentoring took me on for life, they would have balked.

After I graduated from high school, I spent several months deciding what to do with my life while working for and with Hank.

He wasn't married, he didn't have any children, and it seemed he was anxious—or at least very willing—to share the experience of a lifetime with me. Little did I know that his experience of a lifetime was a life of crime. However, Hank was smart, he was apparently well-to-do, and he was never caught. He didn't just teach me to steal over the next few years. He also taught me how *not* to get caught. Apparently, he was very successful at both. I was less successful at the latter. Maybe I was not as smart as him. But also, in his time, criminal investigators only had limited tools like fingerprints to catch thieves.

When I hit the scene of the crime, DNA and wireless technology made my craft less illusive.

Hank was honest with me, and one day, while sipping iced tea in the backyard, he told me how he made a living and that he was willing to mentor me.

I was young, didn't much about life, easily influenced, and didn't know what to do. I didn't like digging ditches. I saw people struggling their whole lives and living in houses eaten up with termites, driving cars that didn't run well, and using lawnmowers that broke down. My perspective on life wasn't that good. If I would have listened to my parents and adopted their worldview, perhaps I would have said no to Hank.

My decision was mostly sensual, meaning based on the senses. He lived in a nice house, had nice cars, had plenty to eat, and often took me to one of the plentiful Galveston restaurants. He didn't seem to have a care in the world.

I told him, "Yes, I'll give it a shot."

What Hank did *not* tell me and what I didn't see (initially) was that he was always alone. He was lonely, with no family and no friends. He purposely avoided any contact with his neighbors. He was a recluse. And he was "running" from the law but hiding in plain sight.

Within a few days of my commitment to Hank, he mentored me on my first job—a heist actually.

I had been in Hank's house many times but never to one particular room. It was his "disguise" room. It was about twenty by twenty feet with no windows. There were shelves on two sides and closets on the other two walls. On the shelves were rubber masks and wigs. He could look like anyone he wanted, from a young man to very old ladies. The clothes matched the character or the "man" needed for the job. He had three-piece suits and homeless rags and everything in between. Most of the clothes he had bought at estate sales, he told me.

He proceeded to put on a mask. And in front of a mirror and a makeup desk, he turned himself from a sixty-year-old man to a forty-year-old construction worker, including coveralls, Carhartt jacket, and aluminum helmet.

Hank had a map of Galveston but not the one you get from Rand McNally. He had ordered the plats (squares) from the USGS. He would order all the topographical maps, tear off the edges, and glue them on one wall of his house. This was way before that was cool or popular.

But Hank did not do that for either of those reasons. He planned every entrance and egress for every job he did, drawing with a pencil or a highlighter the best way in and out. This included the structures and the space between structures. (That would come in handy as I used a motorcycle for getaways later in life.)

When he felt like he knew the area, without ever having been there, he would feel like he was ready for the job. He trained me. He never did physical stakeouts because security cameras would catch you and your license plate. He would have very good maps and study them, which eliminated the need for actual location observation.

It was a cool Wednesday in October when he uncovered one of the mystery cars, which turned out to be a light blue Ford F-150, two-door, straight-six engine. It ran great. We drove to the southwest side of Galveston.

We went to the Bountiful Gardens construction site. All those pyramids and roads were not all built at once. There was a master development plan, but it started small. The property was bought, and temporary portable offices were set up on the edge. People were hired, and construction began.

It was about six miles from Hank's house. We drove farther south, turned around, and approached the construction site from the south. That was another trick that stayed with me for many years.

We went to the Bountiful Garden site, told the guard we were looking for work, and were pointed to the portable office buildings. There were about three, all connected in a horseshoe shape.

We talked to the construction foreman. By "we," I mean Hank. I didn't say a word. Hank asked about work and told them he was an excellent welder who could do regular, TIG, and even aluminum welding. The foreman was impressed and gave Hank an application. Hank limped a little. I wondered if he had hurt his leg the day before. Hank was careful *not* to touch anything, but he sure looked around and observed *everything*. The foreman said there were four hundred men working on the site now, and payday was in two days. (He shouldn't have said that.)

He took a liking to Hank—everybody did—and showed him the other two offices. One was HR, and one was accounting and receiving. Trucks with new material arrived each day. Hank secured me the job to work in receiving right there. I was handed an application on the way out also. I never filled it out.

We drove away, to the south. Out of sight, we turned around and went home, parked the truck in the garage with the door closed, and put the tarp back over it.

That was when Hank told me that the next day, Thursday, at night, we would do our first job. He told me all the things he'd observed:

1. There was no night security, just a fence.
2. The buildings had paper-thin walls.
3. The safe had an electronic lock, which he could open quickly. Hank was a safe expert.
4. The money would have to be there, the day before payday, to meet the payroll.
5. The doors had deadbolts, but the doorjambs were cheap.
6. The AC had window units that could easily be removed from the outside.
7. Curtains or blinds to block the outside view.

He'd also observed where the electricity entered the building, what kind of alarm system or cameras were there, whether the floor had vinyl or carpet, and so on.

Basically, in the short time Hank and I had talked to the foreman, and on our little walk-through, Hank had made a mental map of the buildings. The vinyl squares were one foot each. By counting them, Hank knew the exact width and length of each office building and where things were located. He drew the three buildings and their floor plans on his computer in AutoCAD when he got home and printed them out.

Hank drew our plan of "attack." This was where we would go in, and this was where we would go out. This was where we parked, and we would walk from here. We would commence at 10:00 p.m. Thursday evening. The weather forecast showed heavy rain with low visibility. Perfect for our plan. We didn't really care about seeing or being seen.

The next day, Thursday, at 10:00 p.m., we got in the truck and drove to the construction site as close as the fence would allow. It was dark, and it was raining hard. We wore dark clothing, and the shoes we wore that day went in the trash the next day. We never wore them again. Another trick I learned from Hank: "No shoe or shoeprint left behind."

We wore gloves—rubber surgical gloves inside black nylon gloves. After the job, they went into a small incinerator he kept in his backyard; the neighbors thought it was a barbeque pit.

We parked near the chain-link fence; cut our way through with wire cutters; walked to the office trailers; and, by prying the doorjamb away, forced the door to fly open. Hank went straight to the safe. With a rare earth magnet in the right location, the safe unlocked. And when Hank rotated the large handle in the middle, the door swung open. Four hundred people getting paid $20per hour for forty hours and overtime. There was about $300,000 of cash in that safe, neatly stacked in piles of hundred-and twenty-dollar bills.

Hank had a special bag that looked like an old-fashioned doctor's bag that the money fit in perfectly. That took less than five minutes. Hank was right. There was no security and no alarm system. We did not touch anything else, except on the way out he told me to grab two of the portable radios and a charger. Not only could we hear at our house the commotion the robbery had caused, but we continued to monitor them infrequently to see if there was reason to make a second visit at Bountiful Gardens.

A year or so later, when we needed two vehicles for a job, Hank and I used the same radios to stay in touch with each other. After that job, we sold them to a pawnshop and still got $100each for them. Hank was, let's say, "frugal."

We got home at 11:45 p.m. and counted the money. I had never seen $300,000 in cash before. Hank gave me $500 in twenty-dollar bills, and I went home. I'd never had so much money. I had to hide it in my room; my parents would neither understand nor approve.

I knew my dad would have to work all year for a third of that kind of money, and we'd made three times as much in one night. I was sold on my new career.

I moved out shortly after that and got my own apartment, first in Galveston. But because there was more loot up for grabs in Houston, I moved to Houston after a while. It became a lucrative career—but not always with a happy ending. And I never could relax as much as I thought Hank did.

Hank taught me a lot more tricks of the trade. He showed me how to use disguises. He had limped into the Bountiful Garden office during the job application on purpose; I didn't realize till later that was part of the plan. If the foreman had been suspicious of the applicant being the robber, he would have described him as a man in his forties with a limp, leaving Hank off the radar.

Later, he showed me another room in the house, in the attic, that had all kinds of electronic equipment—expensive, high quality color photocopiers; scanners, label makers, laminators, badge makers, credit card duplicators, cameras, microscope, laptops, ham radios, scanners, and several other gadgets. There were solar panels on the roof, and a small wind generator was attached to the top nook of the house. (The wind always blows in Galveston.) Hank's house was three stories, higher than any other house on the street. It had a round room on the third floor, with windows all around. You could see over the seawall and hear the ocean but also see the water on the other side of the island, the West Bay. A charge controller, lithium twenty-four-volt batteries, and an inverter—uninterruptable power supplies—provided Hank with ample power in case of a grid failure.

Hank introduced me to the traveling car lot. He would continually buy and sell stolen car, and always use one car for only *one* job. He taught me how to stage one or two cars at each location where you lived. Then if you were surrounded and your vehicles were compromised, you could sneak your way to the getaway car and disappear into the sunset.

He told me to invest in gold and to hide the gold in nearby locations. They did not have to be secluded or far away, as long as you had the GPS locations. You would have enough to leave everything behind and make a new start—new residence, new cars, new equipment, new everything. I made use of that training several times, as you will find out in chapter 1.

Thieves usually get caught when they're either in the action of stealing or while bragging when disposing of the stolen items. Hank advised me to talk little about the line of work.

Another thing that might seem insignificant was that *Hank would never take his picture or let anybody take a picture of him or with him.* This turned out to be one of the greatest pieces of advice he gave me.

Much later, as I became Houston's Most Wanted and was sought by the Houston PD, one of the reasons they couldn't find me was that nobody knew what I looked like. There were no pictures of me; consequently, I avoided any form of social media.

That was a result of having no family reunions to go to and avoiding thanksgiving dinners and get-togethers, including weddings and funerals. It made me chuckle years later when I realized the only pictures available of me were mug shots.

Hank told me, as he was mentoring me, that he really was semiretired and would leave everything he owned to me, as he did not have any family. He died exactly three years after our first job. The last thing he told me, on his deathbed, right before his last breath was, "It's a lonely life." Those words haunted me for a long time.

Not only did he leave me the house and all his equipment, but he also had gold stashed on his property and elsewhere on the island. He had $750,000 in the bank. He didn't take it out and hand it to me but, rather, gave me his debit card and pin number before he passed, and I lived comfortably for a long time like that. Keeping his house and his mailing address, of course, gave me access to all his bank correspondence.

Over time, I transferred his money in different accounts in different banks, always keeping the transfers below $10,000 dollars.

I kept the house in Galveston for many years. When I moved to Houston and bought property in the city limits, I rented the house for a while, eventually selling it to the renters, owner financed, which gave me another steady form of cash flow.

Hank also moved among the upper class of the Galveston Medial world. He knew how to dress the part and had convinced most people he was a retired surgeon. One day, he took me with him to a party of the doctors and lawyers of the island. He was able to get information on many of their Mercedes, Corvettes, and Lamborghinis. And with forged keys and knowledge of the cars' locations, he unloaded several high-end cars to the traveling car lot in Houston, pocketing large amounts of money.

I still miss Hank. He was the closer to me than my dad or brother. My life would have taken a whole different turn if I would have nourished a relationship with my father instead, though. Even though Hank mentored me on the wrong path, he did share the best practices of his trade with me, which kept me in money and out of jail for a long, long time.

Hold on for an adrenaline-filled ride.

CHAPTER 2

THE NISSAN FRONTIER TANK

If you *ever* buy a new vehicle, buy a Nissan Frontier! This vehicle proved to be as useful for me as a Sherman Tank was to the Allies in World War I.

And I was literally at war with the law in Houston. No matter where I lived, I always had one car to drive regularly and two vehicles parked as getaway cars in case I needed to make a run for it. They were gassed up, keys hidden, ready to go in the case of an emergency; it was my escape hatch.

There were plenty of times when they came in handy. There's a car dealer in Houston where you can buy a good car, cheap, no title, no paperwork—just pay anywhere from five hundred to a few thousand dollars and drive off, depending on how fancy you want to go. They're all stolen cars, ready to go for any criminal activity you might have planned. I was one of their better customers! This "car lot" was in a different location every night, announced on WhatsApp only; I will describe this in a later chapter.

It was a beautiful sunny day in southeast Texas. My wife, Janet, and I had been grocery shopping at the HEB, not the closest one; I never shop in the neighborhood where I live. I always shop at a variety of grocery stores indifferent parts of town. That was part of the "running" lifestyle. I didn't want a store clerk to get to know me—to recognize me and my shopping patterns. That way, if the police ever questioned her, all she would be able to say was, "I only saw him once." Neither was I unusually friendly and inquisitive or rude with any store clerk; I tried to live under the radar—inconspicuous, unnoticed, just the average Joe.

We returned home with a car full of groceries. The bed of the truck and the back seat were loaded. Those groceries might have actually saved our lives later—as a bullet barrier.

At that time, we lived in an apartment complex on Beltway 8 called the Reserve, City Center North.

The apartment we lived in had two entrances, one in the front and one in the back; both had a numbered code access gate.

We arrived at our apartment. The complex had two ways to get in or out of the secured area. It had a number code access gate on both sides. I would never consider renting where there was only *one* entrance, for fear of being trapped.

There were fourteen buildings in the shape of two large letter Cs; a more extensive C on the outside, circling the whole complex; and a smaller C on the inside, where the administration building, pool, and washateria were located. With that layout, there were actually four ways to get in and out of the complex, and if one approach was blocked, you could always drive through the grass and hit another exit!

To the north of the complex was a high-voltage power line right-of-way, which meant no one would ever build there. There was a dirt track frequented by ATVs right under the power lines and a drainage ditch running beside it. All that made for an excellent possible escape route, either with a four-wheeler or a bike or on foot. If you are very desperate and have to crawl through a drainage ditch, it will take you under roads and sometimes buildings. In a later chapter, I will tell you how I crawled, with my wife, through a ditch under an unsuspecting police car that was part of a "locked down area," stationed there to prevent my escape.

To the west was West View School, a school for children with autism, the only one in the country that specialized in this area. There was an extensive tree line blocking the view of the school from the apartment complex and vice versa. On the other side of the school was a large round dome and, past there, a "castle" built as a youth center for the local church. This could be another way to "melt" into a crowd if need be.

To the south was Hammerly Boulevard. If I couldn't make my getaway on an interstate, I tried to locate my residence close to a four-lane road. On a four-lane road, there usually was ample room, since both lanes weren't always in use. And if both pathways were blocked, there was often a wide shoulder to travel on.

I kept a map of the complex and surrounding roads printed large, four feet by four feet, on the wall by the front door of the apartment. That way, every time I left or hung up my keys, I looked at the map and studied it. I printed it in my mind. In that way, if I ever had to make a quick getaway and men were posted in specific locations, I would have a greater chance of sneaking out and around buildings, bushes, and signs to make a clean escape. Knowledge is key.

I had two cars parked on the outer circle and moved them now and then. If I could make it to one of those cars, my run would be a home run; I'd get to another temporary place to continue my lifestyle of "organizing." In twenty years running around Houston, I did a lot of "organizing."

I thought as a fugitive, and I lived as a fugitive. I enjoyed life, but I knew I was a hunted man. I was ready to disappear at any moment. I had a few gold bars and some rolls of forty Krugerrands hidden on Galveston Island. If I had to leave everything behind, including my apartment and vehicles, I could be rich in a day and start over quickly.

For those of you who don't know what a Krugerrand is, the Krugerrand is a South African gold coin, first minted in 1967 to help market South African gold and produced by the South African Mint. By 1980, the Krugerrand accounted for 90 percent of the global gold coin market. A Krugerrand is about one and a quarter inches in diameter, which makes it a little smaller than a silver dollar and a little larger than a quarter.

You can put forty of them in a paper roll and carry forty thousand dollars with you very inconspicuously. They're easy to carry and easy to hide. No reputable coin dealer will ever turn you away if you want to cash in a Krugerrand. For a criminal like me, it was a very respectable way to walk into a jewelry store and walk out with a thousand dollars in my pocket. After breaking into a judge's house and finding many of them (more about that in another chapter), it became my valuable of choice to hide a large amount of money. When I needed to start over, I would dig some up and be back on my feet in no time.

The Chase

I turned into the north entrance and drove slowly into the circular drive of the vast complex. There were buildings on each side with parking spaces and one assigned parking space for each apartment. Certain parking spots were assigned to visitors.

When I made the left turn going south, something caught my eye. After living a life of crime for so long, I felt like Spider-Man sometimes. I could *feel* when danger was near!

By this time, I had developed an instinct for the unfamiliar. Like a large buck in the East Texas woods who, even if a hunter wears camouflage and scent-covering outfits, will run at the sound of one dead breaking limb under the feet of the hunter, never to be seen again, I was alert!

I made it a habit to know my turf, who was supposed to be there and who was not, what cars people drove, and where they parked. It is amazing what creatures of habit we are. Some always pull in straight; others back in.

The "danger" I was sensitive to was not violence to my person, but the closeness of being caught by the police. So far, my alertness had helped me escape, sometimes in the nick of time.

And there was *one* of those territory markers out of place, one deer scrape on a tree. There was a car I did not recognize—a black Dodge Charger. A man was sitting in it. There was one thing and only one that set off all my Spidey sense alarms.

He looked up!

He should have kept reading his paper and just glanced over it or played with his phone or changed the channel on his radio or loosened his seat belt or anything else. But he did something he should not have done. He looked up.

He looked up, somewhat intently, with a searching, questioning gaze, perhaps a look of recognition. When I looked into his eyes, I knew he had been sent to stake me and that he had that 'gotcha' feeling inside of him. That look alone triggered something inside me.

I had that same instinct as the deer; I sensed who was after me. It wasn't just paranoia, but a gut feeling of being watched, being in someone's scope.

I was in a searchlight and knew he wanted to take me down. But I wasn't going to make it easy on him; I was going to make a run for it!

So I said, "Hold, on honey!"(It was the first of several times I'd say that line that day.)

We circled around to the left and drove back out of the apartment complex through the other exit. From where he was sitting, the guy in the Charger could not have observed us entering the gate; he was too far around the corner from the entrance. So there was a possibility he could have thought we were coming *out* of an apartment and were just going shopping.

But no such luck. My "sense" proved right again! Sure enough, the black car pulled out and started following us. I took a right turn on the Beltway 8 feeder road. He was about a hundred yards behind me when he came out of the complex, trying to be inconspicuous, I guess.

At Hammerly Boulevard, I took the underpass to the left, and on the other side of the beltway. I immediately entered the ramp going north. For those of you not familiar with Houston, Beltway 8 is privately owned and is a toll road. I should have known better! He was on his radio, and I could pick him up on my scanner. It's hard to outrun a radio signal, even with the fastest car! He was calling for backup, but I also heard that he was *not* sure I was the man he was searching for.

It was a busy day, around rush hour, with many cars on the Beltway. I initially kept the speed limit at seventy miles per hour. I could see the black car in my mirror. I hadn't shaken him yet!

It was a black Dodge Charger, typical Houston City Police issue. They modified their cars, usually with reinforced bumpers, lights, computers, and souped-up carburetors. Some even had nitro! This one might have a modified engine, but they'd kept the outside stock. It looked like a normal car; the windows were tinted so you could not see the law enforcement tools. Even the antennas were invisible. They utilized the car radio antenna for their shortwave.

Let me give you the lowdown on the two fighters in the ring before you see who is going to win in the final round. This will give you enough information, perhaps, to place your bets as to who will be the winner.

Ladies and gentlemen, in the left corner is the Nissan Frontier weighing in at 4,200 pounds. With a 6-cylinder, 4.0-liter, 261 horsepower engine, six-speed automatic, disk brakes and 17-inch tires. It is 206 inches long, 73 inches wide.

In the right corner is the Dodge Charger, weighing in at 4,365 pounds with an 8-cylinder, 6.4-liter HEMI, 485 horsepower engine, eight-speed automatic, hydraulic assist disc brakes, 20-inch tires. It is 200 inches long, 74 inches wide.

Place your bets!

If it were a real boxing match, the Charger would have won easily, but it lost! In the battle of the bumpers, the Nissan Frontier ended up winning, much to my surprise! I increased my speed to eighty miles an hour and told my lady," Hang on, honey."

By this time, I was weaving in and out of traffic again and was able to put about ten car lengths between us. If the road were clear, he probably would have caught up with me. But because of the volume of cars, he got caught in between vehicles a few times, which allowed me to "getaway"—at least, almost.

I hit eighty miles an hour, ninety, and then one hundred, and he was still there. A hundred miles per hour puts you in another world. Not only are you in more danger of losing control, but you also are—guess what?'—breaking the law! Duh. Do you think it's breaking the law if you 'e driving with excessive speed trying to get away from the cops for breaking another law? Or is it OK to speed then?

So I was getting away until—remember, I said Beltway 8 is a toll road, and the toll booths were right there ahead of me. There were now two cars in front of me; the toll section was eight lines wide. The black Dodge Charger was ten car lengths behind me. You wonder, Why didn't I take the EZ TAG lanes? Well, I never owned an EZ TAG box, so, through force of habit, I took the cash lane. Big mistake!

Then there was just one car in front of me. Then it was my turn to pay the $1.75 fee or drop the 7 quarters in the slide.

I usually kept the armrest full of change. That's what you do if you live near toll roads. I never considered getting a quick pass box because they can track and build a history file of all your movements. I always paid cash, but not this time!

Right in front of me, on the other side of the bar that raises after you pay were *two black Suburbans*, with four men standing beside them with guns pointed at me!

Remember that, when you run from the cops, a radio signal is always faster than a car.

I told my wife again, "Hold on, honey!"

There were two cars in line behind me, their drivers ready to pay their tolls and head on with their lives. They had no idea what thrills this day would bring them!

I threw the Nissan Frontier in reverse and rammed the car behind me, pushing it back a few feet. The tow hook embedded itself in the bumper and radiator in the car behind me. I always kept a tow hook installed. You might bump your shins on it when you walk around the back of the truck, but if somebody runs into you, the tow hook takes all the damage, and you can usually drive away. But their vehicle looks like somebody stuck their finger in the icing of your birthday cake. All four of the cops started shooting their Glocks and Berettas! Now I was really a hunted fugitive, running from the cops, bullets whizzing around us.

There wasn't enough room to turn around and squeeze through. So I went forward, towards the bullets hitting the windshield! You probably don't know that only a .45 caliber handgun has enough momentum to go through a car windshield. The lighter caliber guns make a loud bang and a nasty indention in the windshield but do not go through. Don't ask me how I found out!

There were at least four men with pistols—no heavy guns. But I wasn't really thinking about what a bullet would do to my flesh. I only had *one* thought—to get out of there ASAP!

One bullet hit the front of the right mirror and went through the plastic. Consequently, the mirror shattered in a thousand pieces. Then the same thing happened to the left mirror! Did they do that on purpose, or were they just bad shots? I was hoping they were rookies and didn't spend a lot of time in the shooting range. Not too many people are accurate with a handheld pistol. A million thoughts went through my mind. My first .22 pistol was so inaccurate I couldn't even hit a refrigerator at twenty-five feet! I traded it in right away for a Ruger 10/22 semiautomatic rifle, an excellent squirrel gun.

I carried a gun in my car, always did, but hadn't ever used it. In all my criminal life, I never had to use a weapon. I never shot or stabbed anybody, never used any violence toward a lawman. So if you are looking for violence in this book, sorry. In one chapter of this book, I will write about violence, but almost all of it happened while I was incarcerated. Back to the gun battle or, better, the hail of bullets; or perhaps car battle would be a better description of the situation at hand.

When I had a few feet between me and the car behind me, I put the truck in reverse again and floored it. When I hit the car behind me, it flew backward about six feet and hit the car behind it. The noise of crashing cars is somewhat unnerving.

The choice between bullets in my body, spending time in jail and prisons, and dents in the Nissan Frontier and the other two cars, was easy. I chose the dents! Here I was, running for my life again, full speed.

I pushed forward again, and this time, I was able to create a little more of a runway. Driving straight towards those cops shooting had me hoping the windshield would hold and that none of them had the smarts to shoot through my radiator. An overheated car does not go very far.

The third time I hit the two cars behind me, I created just enough space for me to turn around. I spun the truck around and started racing against the traffic!

Don't try that at home. The beltway traffic on the west side outside lanes goes south, except for me. If you think weaving in and out of traffic trying to escape the police is hard going *with* the traffic, going against the traffic raised my adrenaline, my blood pressure, the RPMs of the Nissan Frontier, and my wife's volume. I am not sure if she screamed with excitement or if the popping sound of the bullets were ringing fear in her heart.

Believe it or not, the cop in the black Dodge Charger turned around and was *right on my tail.* This guy was good, but I had another trick up my sleeve. We were going ninety-five miles per hour; he was less than a car length behind me and hoping to push me with the corner of his bumper, which could cause my vehicle to spin.

My speed was way above average, and I was passing cars on the left and the right. By passing, I mean they were going south; I was going north. I was whizzing by them faster than they could react, for the most part. There were four lanes, and usually, I could squeeze through a hole, keep up my speed, and try to lose the ankle biter. At least I tried!

He was still on my tail, our engines roaring, and I wanted to lose him badly. I said, "Hold on, honey," for the last time that day and instantly hit my brakes as hard as I could.

The cop did not expect that; it took him totally by surprise. He did not have time to find his brake pedal and, consequently, slammed his Dodge Charger into the back of the Nissan Frontier. The tow hook again did its job, piercing the radiator and releasing a lot of green hot steam.

It wasn't exactly hitting a brick wall, but pretty close to it. I'd wondered what would happen myself! To my surprise, it had the desired effect, even though the Nissan Frontier was quite a bit lighter and smaller than the Charger, the maneuver shut the Charger down.

Not just that, but a lot more happened!

I could not observe it myself, because I was speeding away into *very* startled traffic. I didn't have time to look into the only mirror not shot to pieces—the center one; my thoughts were racing as fast as the car. I almost felt sorry for these poor Beltway 8 commuters, who suddenly had a gold Nissan Frontier barreling towards them with a speed that, to them, appeared to be 160 miles per hour. I was on top of them almost before they could see me.

So I couldn't see what was unfolding behind me, but my lady could, and she kept me informed with loud, high-pitched commentary:

"*The Dodge is stopped*!"

"*It caught fire*!"

"*The doors are jammed*!"

"*His buddies in the Suburbans are stopped to help him get out*!"

We heard the same cry of despair on my ham radio police scanner. In every car I ever drove, I installed a ham radio. I did not have a ham license, but the false aliases I used did. All the neighboring county police frequencies were programmed in that ham radio. I could hear they were angry, desperate, and very eager to catch me! But they were even more anxious to save their buddy from a burning car.

My sudden stop that caused the crash between us did them in. I'd never thought it would be such a successful maneuver. The battle of the bumpers was won by the Nissan Frontier—the score, Nissan Frontier1, Dodge Charger 0, by TKO.

One "little" hit, and the doors jammed, and the car caught fire.

If you're seriously thinking about buying a dependable car, one that holds up to bullet holes, being driven backward into multiple vehicles, and winning a crash battle with a Dodge, then *buy a Nissan Frontier*, OK?

They must be built like a Sherman tank! The internal bracing must be designed by highly qualified mechanical engineers. Or perhaps they're a little more liberal with their metal in hidden places than the Dodge Corporation.

The Charger could have led to the death of the cop, and that certainly was not my intention. I was glad he didn't die, and his colleagues got him out safely. During the whole twenty-five years in my criminal "career," I never shot or stabbed or committed violence to any person. I did not shoot at law enforcement people. I became an expert in slipping out of their dragnet. I did point my gun at someone, one time. I will tell you about that in a later chapter.

I did a lot of stealing, robbing, wheeling, and dealing. But I never did drugs or violence during a crime. There will be some descriptions of violence in this book. But most of it happened while I was locked up *in* prison. And every time it was because I had to defend my life and/or status in prison. I have seen a lot more violence *in* the prison than out, I'm sorry to say.

So, with the Charger burning and then all the police vehicles stopped in the middle of Beltway 8, the commotion on the freeway was substantial. This all cause an instant "parking lot" of cars, which allowed me a relatively clean getaway.

But my adrenaline told me I didn't have much time. Remember the speed of the radio? I knew I had to get off the highway and dump this hot car, so I did. The Houston police department, with a budget more significant than most Fortune 500 corporations, had several helicopters in their fleet. And I was pretty sure one of their 16 Schweizer MD500 helicopters was hurling toward me at ninety miles per hour post haste!

I took the next exit, which, for the vehicles I encountered, was an *entrance* ramp. Again, I was skirting around very surprised Houstonians who were trying to go south on Beltway 8. ButI went too fast going around the corner, lost control, jumped the curb, and hit a light post head-on. The galvanized lamppost was securely mounted down with heavy bolts to a large cylinder of cement about a foot up from the ground. The bolts held, and for a second, the lamp just swayed back and forth. Metal fatigue set in quickly, and on the last backward sway, like in a comic strip, the lamppost slowly folded over, and lay straight across the front bumper and the roof of my truck. It made a significant dent in the roof between Janet and me. *And* the engine died!

So, not exactly up a creek without a paddle, but under a light post without an engine! We were quite surprised, hmm, stuck and scared. Running would not have gotten us very far, and the chopper was on the way for sure. The Houston police do not take lightly to the destruction of their fleet on purpose by fleeing criminals.

I turned the key, and to my surprise, the engine cranked. I backed the Nissan Frontier from under the light post. It moved backward, dropping the streetlight right in front of us, and we were free. The *tank* kept on running! Not only was it badly banged up in the rear, but the front and roof were sporting a big wave in the sheet metal. But we were rolling.

I pulled into a shopping mall parking lot, called a taxi company, and told him I had a family emergency, and I'd pay him $200 if he could be there in two minutes. He was there in one. We abandoned the Nissan Frontier, our faithful tank. I still miss it.

The police helicopter blades were whirring overhead with their searchlights looking for my car as we jumped into the taxi van. As we slid the doors shut, the taxi driver asked us, "I wonder what's going on?"

I told him, "I think they're looking for somebody." I didn't volunteer the information that somebody was *us*.

We let the taxi drop us a distance from the apartment, and believe it or not, there was nobody there or watching it. We emptied it out, using one of my spare cars and deserted the apartment.

It looked like negligence that someone did not have it staked it out. I guess the brave guy in the Dodge Charger didn't have time to radio in that he'd started the chase at my apartment and that it was the correct place for a stakeout.

Perhaps he was too busy weaving in and out of traffic chasing me the wrong direction on Beltway 8. Or probably he was preoccupied with almost being fried in his Charger. Whatever the reason, he neglected to mention to his superiors that he'd found out I lived in that apartment complex.

We had ample time to pack up our clothes and money, gold coins, falsification equipment, fake IDs, and whatever else could have traced back to us. We threw the copy machines and fax machines in the apartment dumpster. There was hardly anything left in the apartment when we locked the door.

Time to go back to Galveston, where my secret Jean Lafitte inspired gold stash was. (Treasure map in the back of the book!) I dug up a roll of Krugerrands, and we spent the night at the Commander. We already had our eyes on the next place, near the galleria, a penthouse, top floor with a good view.

I would pick up my spare cars later, wearing a disguise and riding my Harley with my wife on the back.

See you, next time, Detective. I'm glad you didn't get burnt!

CHAPTER 3

THROUGH THE WALLS

"No way out" didn't really fit my lifestyle. Perhaps that could be said only of the time I spent in prison—during which I always was looking for a way out. But if you'd spent only one Christmas at home in the last twenty-five years and all the other Christmases were in some prison or jail, then you'd understand.

This time, though, it was close. I was blocked in the back and the front by the Houston SWAT Team. Neither the backdoor nor the front door key would help me this time. So I had to figure out what to use as a key and how to construct my own door.

I was living in a townhouse at this time. These townhouses were all exactly the same on the inside. But on the outside, the architect had used his creativity and given all of them different fronts. Some had a small fake balcony arching out from the top bedroom window. Some had shingles coming from the top of the roof, running down all the way to the ground floor, leaving cut-outs of small alcoves for the living room windows and the front door. It gave the appearance of diversity from the outside, but on the inside, they were the same. This gave me a great advantage for the endeavor I was about to undertake.

All the front doors were different also. Wherever I bought or rented a house, I replaced the front door with a solid steel door. This front door was not only made out of two steel plates with insulation in between, but it also had bars all the way through like a safe. The bars locked in the frame at all four sides; this door could not be taken out by two men with a police ram.

When you locked this steel, solid core door, three pins about an inch thick came out of the side of the door to the right and left and inserted themselves in reinforced holes in the doorjambs.

The backyards were small, and there was no back door, but you could access them through the double sliding glass door in the breakfast nook. Instead of grass, the backyard was concrete tiles. This suited me just fine—no lawn to mow and a solid bottom. We had a sizeable cast-iron barbeque pit with a smoker attached. Janet could cook, fry, or smoke just about anything and make it smell and taste sumptuous.

The front yard was a postcard joke, as wide as the house, with a small white picket fence on each side, separating the neighbor's similarly tiny front yard. The mailman had to walk about ten steps for each house to deposit the letter and magazines in the mail slot in the front doors.

Our townhouse was in the middle of a row of twelve. I purposely rented this one and not the one in the corner. You will find out why in a minute.

The front and back walls are yours, but the walls on both sides of the townhouse are co-owned by you and the neighbor. To my frustration, you often could hear the neighbors' TV or radio blaring through the walls. Well, there was a positive side to having thin walls, I realized. The key didn't have to be so heavy.

The SWAT team was waiting; cars blocked the road on both sides! The Special Weapons and Tactics vehicle with the big white SWAT letters on the side was parked right in front of my apartment. They were ready to swat me like a fly on the wall.

How they'd found me or knew I lived there and was home, I never figured out. Perhaps somebody ratted on me, possibly my ex-girlfriend! She had proven to be a Judas before. She'd stolen from me and, in several other significant ways, had proven to be a liar. (Please give me a paper towel to wipe the bitter taste out of my mouth.)

What the cause was I did not know. I did see that I had *very* little time to get out of there; the trap was about to close.

SWAT would not hesitate to break the glass in the double sliding doors in the back. That was no easy access either; I had replaced the glass with safety glass. Two layers of glass with plastic in between would not shatter or crack very far. It would hang in the frame and give me some time to think of a solution.

The front door was a lot harder to break, but they would try. A fortress is only as strong as its weakest point, and this townhouse fortress had many weak points. They were about to come in; I didn't have much time to make an escape.

I did have a sledgehammer.

It proved to be a formidable key.

I realized that the front and back were blocked and that there was no James Bond helicopter to pull me off the roof and whisk me away! I could not dig a tunnel like a mole, and up or down were out of the question also. That didn't leave but two options in a three-dimensional world, to get out of this predicament.

If the front and back were blocked, the up (ceiling) wasn't an option, and the down (basement) wasn't an option, that only left right and left. I picked left.

Standing in the living room, I grabbed my backpack, closed the lid of my laptop to put it inside, and walked to the bedroom.

In the bedroom, I took my cell phone from the top of the nightstand and put it in my pocket. From the drawer, I grabbed the roll of Krugerrands and threw them in my backpack also, slung the backpack over my back and locked the bedroom door. Every second I could delay the determined men with the heavy body armor counted.

I picked up the Ace twenty-pound sledgehammer, with the thirty-six-inch hickory handle that had never been used for anything. It was leaning against the wall of my bedroom; its sole purpose was to be my last resort, my master key, so to speak.

I raised the sledgehammer and drove it through the Sheetrock between the left side of the bed and the closet; it was about six feet of space there.

Wall number 1, neighbor number 1

Bam! The sledgehammer made a large cut on my side of the Sheetrock, about three feet long.

Bam, I hit it again, missed the studs, and now penetrated the neighbor's Sheetrock in his living room. I had no idea if he was home, but he was in for a *big* surprise if he was, a visit from an anxious and scary neighbor.

Previously, I had scouted the walls with a stud finder and knew exactly where the studs were. I knew how to get out of the bedroom if I needed to. And if you studied the opposite side of your apartment, you also knew where you would end up on the other side if you tried this. I was confident there was a way of escape, but it was not a conventional line of travel, to say the least.

Sure enough, the neighbors were home—a man and his wife, peacefully sitting on their La-Z-Boys, enjoying another delightful rerun of *The Jerry Springer show*.

If they were not shocked by the confessions of the endless stream of insane people with dysfunctional relationships, they were in for a shock now!

In a cloud of Sheetrock dust, noise, and fragments, a man crashed through their wall and walked into their life—a determined man with a sledgehammer!

They were stunned, frozen, glued to their La-Z-Boys.

I did not give them a formal greeting; I didn't have time that day. They really didn't know me at all. In the line of work I was in, it was better *not* to socialize with your neighbors; the less they knew, the better. That was the first time I'd been face-to-face with them, and my face was covered in white powder.

What would you do if a man came into your living room through the wall holding a sledgehammer with a fierce look on his face? I told them, "Don't move!" And they did not. The guy was not very big, his lady friend was huge, and they were too shocked and scared to move an inch. They just kept their eyes glued on me.

I kept on going. I ran to *their* bedroom and used the same modus operandi. Their bed was located in the same spot, but there was a full-length oval mirror where my new front door was fixing to be. I jerked it to the ground, and the mirror shattered. I wedged the frame under the doorknob, jamming the other side of the mirror frame against the wall. A few more seconds of delay could mean freedom or prison time for me.

I raised the twenty pounder again, in the neighbor's bedroom now; there was more determination in my mind, and I let the hammer come down hard.

Wall number 2, neighbor number 2

Bam! This time, the hammer made a hole through both walls at once. It was a good thing the contractors had followed the blueprint to a T, as I raised the hickory handle one more time. I let it come down hard, and now had enough room to step into the second house of cards.

Nobody home except two cats! They were terrified and clawed their way across the living room carpet; slid, legs flying, across the vinyl in the kitchen; and crashed into the kitchen cabinets and dishwasher. I had no time to observe them. The thigh-slapping laugh had to wait until the SWAT monkey was off my tail.

I ran to the bedroom, hammer raised. Bummer, a bookshelf blocked my way! The bookshelf was an IKEA masterpiece. Not only was it in the exact spot where I wanted to penetrate the Sheetrock in my hasty retreat, but the shelves were also chock-full of books.

The top shelves were smaller, paperbacks; the bottom shelves had the largest books. An old *Encyclopedia Britannica*, yellowed with age, was on the bottom. And in between was anything from *Reader's Digests* to old copies of *National Geographic*. One shelf was full of atlases, from Rand McNally to Travelocity. One shelf had bibles, King James versions, black, red, and brown.

There was one colossal bible; on a separate pedestal, it looked like it was from the seventeenth century. It was almost afoot wide, about six inches thick and a foot and a half tall, closed with brass locks. A beautiful specimen for a collector, probably the oldest book I had ever seen! I made a mental note to perhaps come back for that one later. It seemed valuable and easy to carry.

For a moment, I thought of the value and where I could sell it, but it was a little too large to take with me through the Sheetrock doors, which I was not done creating.

I saw a six-volume commentary of Matthew Henry and a ten-volume commentary of Keil and Delitzsch. One shelf was full of scrapbooks, very colorful.

You probably wonder how I could make all these detailed observations when I was in escape mode running from an elite team of criminal catchers.

It always astounded me that I could remember every minute detail during the most dangerous times of my life when I was running from the cops. My mind would race a hundred miles per hour when trying to make it out of a seemingly impossible situation; likewise, my perception would increase; my vision would be sharper. I could see the shelves, the individual titles. If I recognized a title, I would remember the author, some of the contents of the book, when I had read it, and what it had meant to me—all that in a flash! I had only one thing on my mind. To get out of there as soon as possible, but that thought raced past books, covers, titles, pages, words, contents, and meanings.

If the books did not fill up a section of shelves, then there were bookends, some made out of simple sections of brown steel, some made out of solid brass with matching duck heads. Some were made of black marble in the shape of horses raring up.

IKEA was usually made out of sections, like Lego, perfectly fit together but not necessarily attached; I was hoping it was not! I climbed on a chair and pulled hard on the top of the second section. I had to lean on it with all my might! It slowly moved towards me, coming forward a few inches. I pulled harder and strained. The top was now a foot from the wall. I knew that, with a little more effort, it would come to the point of no return. Some of the books started sliding forward.

Bang, the second IKEA section came crashing to the floor! I jumped out of the way just in time. The side of the section brushed against me, exposing the Sheetrock. Oh, happy day, another spot for me to make a door! Let's make a deal. What is behind Sheetrock number 3?

Only the sledgehammer could tell me. Hammer up, hammer down. I was leaving the scared cats alone.

Wall number 3, neighbor number 3

Bam! I hit the Sheetrock hard, made a four-foot gash, hit it again, and came through the insulation wiring and the Sheetrock on the other side but met some resistance there.

What irony—that neighbor had put a bookshelf on the other side also. But this one was not IKEA and not made of many sections but, rather, just one. Made of solid oak, dark wood, it did not break; I had to push it over. I leaned against it, and I fell through the Sheetrock! I fell with the shelf across a hallway, where it came to a stop at about a forty-five-degree angle, entirely blocking the bathroom door.

Somebody was in there, and I probably scared the poop out of him literally. Can you picture yourself taking a dump in the comfort of your own home, and a bomb goes off? Not out of your rear end but from the neighbor's house into yours, and your perfectly arranged shelf comes crashing toward your bathroom door and locks you in permanently!

Good thing, the SWAT team was on its way to help this unsuspecting neighbor out of a nasty predicament. And it probably was a plus they were locked in there. If I did not scare them to death by coming through the wall with a hammer and a piece of furniture, a group of men with helmets and body armor certainly would!

This house had a different layout. The bathroom where I'd locked the owner in was not where it was supposed to be. They had done some serious renovation. The doors were wider, and there were no thresholds. It did not make sense until I saw an electric wheelchair and hand railings mounted on some of the walls. I'd just broke into an invalid person's house! How low could you get? At least I was not there to steal anything. I was just passing through.

The remodeled floor plan disoriented me somewhat. I ran around the corner. In all the other apartments, this would have been a bedroom. In this apartment, there was a full open kitchen, right next to it a wall, and behind the wall a huge shower, large enough to roll a wheelchair in. This presented somewhat of a conundrum.

In all the apartments before, I had been able to make a wall in the same place, bust the Sheetrock between two studs in the wall. In this house, there was a tiled shower.

I was determined not to be delayed by the change in scenery. Remember, my escape plan was most eminent! My hope was that the Americans with Disability Act was only used to change the internal dimensions of the apartment and that they'd left the framing the same. Usually, if it was government work, it was only superficial. The studs were there, I hoped. Sure enough, they were right where they should be.

This time I did not *raise* my trusty twenty-pound companion. Instead, I stood with my left side against the tiles right under the showerhead; held the sledgehammer way to my right, waist level; and pulled it around me like the ring around Saturn, hitting the tiles with all my might.

Wall number 4, neighbor number 4

Bam! I knew that you *cannot* attach tiles to regular Sheetrock. You have to buy the special hardy plank material, which is a little tougher, somewhat waterproof, and holds the tiles in place. If you use regular Sheetrock to attach tiles, they will start dropping on you like flies, literally. I have seen some sloppy contractor jobs where the showers would melt.

The contractor would make an estimate, do the tile job, get paid, and leave behind a beautiful shower—but also leave town and change phone numbers. The first time the unsuspecting homeowner took a shower, the walls collapsed around him. A good tile layer is worth his weight in gold.

All these facts were racing around in my head as I hit the tiles over and over. This one would take a little more effort. I hit it ten times—then eleven and twelve. The tiles exploded all around me. Small glass-like shards flew around my head and stuck in my hair. Sections fell down. There was no insulation behind that wall; the neighbor's Sheetrock was exposed. I broke a waterline, the hot one. Hot water started shooting up the wall between the two apartments, bouncing off the ceiling and running down it like an upside-down dripping lake.

I had to get out of there quickly now, or I would be soaked and have second-degree burns.

Bang, bang!

It only took two more hits to make a slit through the other side big enough for me to observe the interior decorating skills of the next neighbor.

I cut my pants and scraped my leg on the exposed sharp edges of the tiles. My greatest worry was leaving DNA on the wall there. There was not enough time to make an ideally three foot-by-seven-foot opening and frame it and hang a new door. All I had was my faithful twenty pounder, a very awkward saw at most!

The hole on the shower side was just big enough for me to crawl through. The wall on the other side was thin and flimsy in comparison and allowed me quick access to the next townhouse.

There was a widow lady in the kitchen, making tea. When she heard the commotion, she came waddling to the hallway where I was making my watery entrance, the teapot still in her hand.

She saw me, covered in white powder from several Sheetrock escapades. My shirt was soaking wet and glittering with the sharp edges of tile that covered me like I'd been hit with a spray can of snow leaves on a fake Christmas tree. She dropped the tea kettle and fainted. I felt sorry for her and hoped she hadn't had a heart attack, but I didn't have time to comfort her or to give her mouth-to-mouth resuscitation. I figured the SWAT team would be here shortly attending to all her needs. She'd probably wind up moving to a nursing home, where there was less danger of men with hammers walking through walls!

I walked to the bedroom, my sledgehammer key quite effective now and turned its sheetrock keyhole four times.

I knew where to make the hole and how to hit the wall in just the right spot to make my getaway as efficient as possible.

The old lady's bedroom was sparsely decorated. She had an old iron, twin-size bed with the headboard against the wall, painted red with a white crochet bedspread. The pillows were arranged neatly, like no one ever slept there.

No wonder she'd fainted! Her perfectly ordered world had come thundering down in thirty-seconds. She would need more than a cup of tea now.

No nightstand but a swag lamp attached from the ceiling, hanging about where I needed to make my grand exit. I jerked it off the ceiling and threw it on the bed. Sparks flew as I ripped out the wires, shorted them out, and blew a fuse. The bedroom became dark except for the outside light coming through the curtains.

Bam.

Wall number 5, neighbor number 5

The Sheetrock seemed soft, perhaps because I'd had such a struggle with the previous apartment tile wall! This was easy in comparison. I held the hammer waist high and pushed it forward like a battering ram. The wall caved in. I pushed it again. The wall caved out. Five or six hits, and I could walk between the yellow studs, stepping over the wiring in the wall.

A new living room, a new surprise. *Honey, I'm home*!

No one was home. There was a Longhorn cap lying on the living room table. I put it on and made my way to the front door this time. I brushed off my pants, the white powder making a cloud of dust that came off easily.

There was a coat rack by the front door. I grabbed a nylon jacket. It had the same Hook'em Horns logo. It seemed fitting, since I'd made my way through five walls like a bull in a china cabinet. Wearing the Bevo logo would make a fitting end to my Sheetrock escapades.

In total, I went through five walls. I was at the end of the block. The next wall would have been the brick wall on the outside of the townhouses, and that would have been a tough job even with a sledgehammer.

I figured that, since I was now five houses removed from my apartment, I would not attract a lot of attention leaving "my" apartment.

I casually walked out the front door. Looking to the right, I saw cop cars with flashing lights, the SWAT van, many men in uniform, and curious neighbors milling around nervously. First, I stood there in front of the door, like all curious neighbors do when there is some form of commotion.

After about a minute of "staring at the cops," I turned left on the sidewalk and made my way to my "stashed" car. The key was under the bumper in a magnetic box. I opened the door, cranked it, and disappeared into the Houston traffic.

Another successful escape by Houston's Most Wanted!

I did not have a chance to prepare or carry much with me this time, just my laptop and valuables. I did lose some valuable equipment. By this time, I was big into falsifying licenses and cashing hot checks. I did this by either wearing a simple disguise to throw off the security cameras or by letting other hands cash them for me.

I was on the run again! Besides having two cars parked for emergencies like this, I always had a "safe" house prepared also—an apartment or townhouse rented under a false name, utilities paid, ready to go in a case like this. I just "moved" and went on. It wasn't a carefree lifestyle, but at least today, I was *not* in the county jail.

I drove straight to Galveston Island, bought a GPS at a local pawnshop and a little shovel. I went to my buried treasure between the Commander and my favorite Mexican Restaurant, dug up another roll of Krugerrands, and had forty grand to make my next move!

I was getting tired of running.

CHAPTER 4

THE LOADED JUDGE

A Mexican gang connection told me, "The judge is dead. His house is loaded. Go help yourself." The reason they gave me the tip was a return on an investment I'd made a few years ago.

I was locked up in the county jail, right on the southeast border of Texas and Mexico. I was only in that jail for two days before they extradited me back to Houston. The first day I was there, I was in the food line at 4:00 a.m. In front of me was a Crips gang member; in front of him was R. Espinoza. The chow hall is a large room with tables, bolted to the floor and round tables with four seats attached. But the only way to enter the chow hall was through a narrow passage. On your left was the counter where you got your food; on the right, there was a metal railing, separating you from the main area. The only way to get there was to go all the way through the line and get your food.

I saw the Crips guy in front of me raise his hand; his intention was to plunge it into the neck of the Mexican guy in front of him. Fights often broke out in the chow hall, as that was one of the few places where the population mingled; they were kept separated in different pods (areas) the rest of the time. In his hand was a four-inch-long round shank, tied to his hand with a rag. He was fixing to plunge this shank in the neck of the guy in front of him. If that would have happened, and if he would have been able to stab him like that, it would have severed an artery in his neck; he would have bled to death right there in front of me. There was no way an officer would be able to be there soon enough to help him. The Crips guy knew all this; that was why he planned to attack him in this place and at this time.

Even though I was considered a hardened professional criminal, I never did violence to any men. And to see a guy be murdered in front of me without acting, especially since I had the ability to, was too much and violated even my conscience. I had to do something, even if it meant getting in big trouble, getting a case, perhaps discipline, or time added to my sentence.

I reacted by grabbing the Crips guy's wrist that held the knife and slamming it against the iron metal railing. With my adrenaline flowing, I did not realize how fast and hard his wrist hit the rail, and it broke his wrist. Because of that, he was not able to fulfill his sinister plan. The guards quickly reacted. *Fight*! *Fight*!

At that point, everybody in the chow hall knew to hit the deck and lie on the floor facedown. The only one screaming in agony was the Crips member, and he was proven guilty because the shank was still attached to his hand.

The Crips member was given an additional charge of aggravated assault with a deadly weapon and attempted murder. I was given a case (evaluation for further discipline) initially, handcuffed, and put in solitary for a few hours. But shortly after that, I was interviewed by an investigative committee and actually commended for preventing a murder. I did get ten days in solitary for my heroic behavior—go figure.

What I didn't know was that the guy whose life I saved, Espinoza, was a lieutenant in the gang. This very violent gang did not want to be called M&M and be associated with sweet candy. They were far from sweet—bitter is a better word—and a very large, dangerous, and active gang in the prison system in the southern part of the United States, ruthless in their enforcement. They were notorious for killing, beheading, and hanging the headless corpse from overpasses.

Lieutenant R. Espinoza and I became instant friends. I spent the whole next day in his pod (a wing in a prison building with about sixty beds) and, there, found out his rank and status in the gang. He never moved from the chair behind his desk. Other inmates brought him his food, his games, his towels, his cigarettes, and whatever else he wanted or needed. All he had to do was say the word; every inmate in that jail seemed to be under his command and loyal to him.

Mr. Espinoza was highly respected in the Mexican gang, and he sent word to the Houston associates that I'd saved his life and was to be trusted and rewarded accordingly!

I was released about a month after that. During my last arrest, the officers who'd processed me had made several mistakes, legal technicalities. My case was dropped, and I was allowed to go home, back to Houston.

One of the elected judges—let me withhold his name, but you likely know him; perhaps you even voted for him—was well off and lived in an affluent neighborhood. The Mexican gang usually had cheats, snipes, and informers everywhere. The maid was from Mexico and was on their payroll; also, she knew everything about the inside of the house. She had her own apartment on the property and took care of the family, cooking and cleaning and spying. The yard crew also was aware of the fact that it behooved them to cooperate with La eMe; they knew everything about the outside of the house, the garages, the vehicles, and the comings and goings of the judge.

That was why, when the judge died and his house became fair game, they referred it to me. They gave me the address, told me the judge was dead and that the house was loaded, and dibs on the house as a reward for protecting their lieutenant.

I don't think they knew how rich the judge actually was. I was able to clip coupons from that house for a long time—all for preventing the lieutenant's untimely demise in that chow line.

On my first trip there, I scouted out the upscale neighborhood. The houses were large with larger lots. Every house was on an acre lot, about two hundred by three hundred feet. Most homes were set towards the back of the lot. Almost all had circular driveways; some were lined with meticulously maintained shrubbery. Most of them could easily afford a permanent yardman. They were most likely underpaid, illegal workers who stayed in an improved shed or caretakers building in the backyard and also keeping an eye on the house in the absence of the owner.

The house was worth over a million. Of course, I'd never been there before. In my profession, it was not a normal occurrence to be friends with county judges or to visit them for any social reasons. The only time I'd have seen this guy would have been when I was standing in front of a big wooden desk, and he was behind it holding a wooden gavel. Eventually, he would be hitting that gavel on a sound block and pronouncing something that ended with the words, prison, jail, or years or any combination of those words.

Judges usually have a security detail, often one police officer sitting in a cop car right in front of the house. The policeman would be smoking or playing with his cell phone, listening to his radio while keeping his eye peeled for guys like me or worse. That decrease in the likelihood of his being robbed improved the chance of him accumulating lots of expensive stuff—and leaving it all for me. I would have thanked him if I could.

It took me a few trips to haul the loot back to my place, and it certainly was worth my time. I almost got caught on the last trip, and I lost my car in the process and my wife for a few days. (I'll tell you more of that later.)

The house was a beautiful two-story house with a porch along the front and four white columns going all the way to the roof. The front door was actually two doors that met in the middle, making an arch at the top. In each of the doors was a small one-foot stained glass window. There was an angel design in each one; with light blue wings, flowing white robes, and yellow hair, they faced each other.

The house extended left and right, evenly on each side of the door. It looked like it had a large foyer with a winding, wall-hugging staircase on each side of the foyer. This kind of staircase would make an excellent background for wedding pictures. I could imagine my wife and I standing on the top balcony, with twelve bridesmaids in rainbow pastel standing on the left staircase and sharp-looking guys in tuxes on the right staircase. But it was a pipedream that was not and would never be my life.

There were three windows on each side of the house; the front door was inset a little. The house was red brick, all the way to the top, with a beautiful pattern of some bricks sticking out a little bit and some recessed. The bricklayer who had built this house must have worked on Rice University's administration buildings also. The patterns in this house were very similar to Rice but on a much smaller scale.

In a lot of houses, the left side appears to be living area but is actually the garage, where the driveway goes to the right of the house and makes a sharp left turn into the garage. What appears to be a place where you enjoy the air-conditioning and beautiful carpet is actually a slab where you park your car.

In this house, the left and right sides were both living areas; the total living area was about twenty-five thousand square feet. The garage of this house was in the back, attached to the kitchen area. You could drive on the right side of the house and park on a large concrete area in front of the four-car garage. There was plenty of space to turn around. It also allowed me to park my car without being visible from the road. There was an eight-foot brick wall along each side and back of the property.

How I obtained entrance to the house

I drove up the driveway, took a sharp left behind the house, and parked my black, four-door Nissan Frontier as close to the corner of the house and the attached garage as I could. Where I was parked assured me my vehicle would not be visible from the road. Thanks to the large brick wall around the entire back of the property, the neighbors could not see me either. All this allowed me to park my car, break in the house, take my time, and load up my car without any of the neighbors seeing what I was doing, and it was very convenient for me to come back to several times.

There were no security cameras, but there was an alarm system from a national alarm system supplier. But if I see that blue and white sign in your front yard, you pretty much invite me to come relieve you of your pretty stuff.

I put on a pair of skin-colored latex gloves, not wanting to leave any fingerprints during my social visit to the judge. I placed a suction cup on the glass and used a circular glass cutter to give me clean access to the inside knobs of the back door. I stuck my hand through the hole and unlocked the door. If there were deadbolts, I would have used my lock pick kit, but there was only one lock that was horizontal, locked. I turned it a quarter turn and heard a familiar "click." From then on, I was free to roam and made good use of my privileged access. After I opened the back door, I had about thirty seconds to disarm the system.

I opened the back door and started counting in my head—*thirty, twenty-nine, twenty-eight, twenty-seven …*

Within a few steps, I was in front of the alarm control next to the black refrigerator.

Twenty-six, twenty-five, twenty-four …

I loosened four Phillips screws and tried to pry the bottom clips.

It would not have helped to remove the triple-A batteries, as there's usually a watch battery on the circuit board that continues to trip the alarm without a display on the green LCD screen.

Twenty-three, twenty-two, twenty-one, twenty, nineteen, eighteen ...

Finally, the cover popped off. It took longer than usual.

During my second stay in the prison, my cellie happened to be a professional burglar, who mentored me in the fine art of disabling alarm systems. He had been a career criminal all his life and made a "good" living. During his illustrious career, people started installing more and various alarm systems.

He said, if he had to keep up with the Joneses, he would have to keep up with how the Joneses protected their stuff.

He schooled me in PIR (passive infrared) motion detection), window magnets, floor sensors, infrared beams, and silent alarms. When a new alarm system became available, he was usually the first customer who had one installed! During the installation, he asked a lot of questions. You would not believe what detailed information the professionals are willing to disclose.

To them, he was just a very inquisitive customer, who wanted the best protection available. And what guy does not like to brag about his job and how his product is so much better than the competitor? They would even tell him why. Then, as soon as the installer left, he reverse engineered it to learn from it and to find its weak points.

As soon as he removed the brand "A" alarm system, he would order one from another security company and go through the same thing. They never asked why there were screw holes in the same places where they installed their more superior protection.

After his Alarm Systems 101 class, I felt a lot more confident to continue my "help yourself" career. Immediately upon my release from prison, I went to Home Depot and Lowes and bought any and every kind of do-it-yourself home alarm system controller. I took them apart and studied them as my mentor had told me to do. I studied how they were put together and how to open them up. I found where the circuit board was and how the wires attached to them. The manual even told you the color representation, which was very convenient because it showed you what color the "trip" wires were—which ones to cut.

Most of them were very similar and quite simple. No surface-mounted technology, just resistors and capacitors standing on their little silver soldered posts on their little green boards.

My mentor was right. There were usually only two wires you had to cut. But it had to be those two, and they had to be cut both at the same time. If you cut just one, the other one would trigger the alarm. There was only one different brand. And if you wanted to disable it, you had to install a clip or a piece of wire inside two open contacts and leave them there. I practiced and practiced, like Michael Jordan practiced his free throw, until I could open the alarm controller, find the right wire or resistor, clip it off, and disable the alarm in about twenty seconds. An alarm disabled during the day kept the lawmen away.

This alarm, partly because of the odd location next to the fridge, was a little harder to get to.

Seventeen, sixteen, fifteen, fourteen, thirteen, twelve …

I could see the circuit board.

Eleven, ten, nine, eight …

I had my orange-handled clippers in my mouth.

Seven, six, five, four, three …

I separated the two wires and clipped them off.

The screen went dead; sweat was running down my forehead into my eyes. That was cutting it too close. Two seconds to spare! Then a screen would have started blinking in this firm's headquarters. It was a judge's house; I was sure they had it flagged for high priority, perhaps with an immediate alarm at the local police station! Some of them had strobe lights and speakers hooked up outside. All of those bells and whistles were avoided with the proper application of a one-dollar implement bought at Harbor Freight Tools.

I gave my wife, Janet, our all-clear signal and blew her a kiss. We kept the romance going no matter how I put the meat on the table, and she liked it this way. I kept thinking about what an amazing woman she was. She promised me she would follow me anywhere, and she did. Even at breaking and entering, she was "by my side," so to speak, or perhaps better, a close second.

The life of a criminal can get very lonely; you usually have nobody to share it with. Especially when you end up in prison, there is nobody who cares. There was an exception to this; there was a particular group who seemed to care. But I did not associate much with them, not until much later in life. When I was locked up, my faithful wife, Janet, would write to me at least once a week and come visit me as often as she could. She kept putting money on my books, so I would not feel like a poor man. Usually, I had close to a thousand dollars on my books at all times. Any more would have looked suspicious, but I will write a whole lot more about prison life in a later chapter.

Janet was amazing, I always thought of her as an Indian woman in an American body. She was always by my side, always willing to do what I wanted. Sexually, physically, food wise, anytime, anywhere, she was ready to satisfy my needs. She would cook anything I wanted to eat, and she was an excellent cook. She was an expert in using spices to make any meal a culinary experience, like Uncle Chris and Tony Chachere's. She is beautiful and a good buddy, and during this break-in, she was my shadow, my faithful companion. What more does a man need than a woman to love and a partner in crime?

We were in.

"Organizing" the stuff!

I had my work cut out for me in this enormous mansion. Janet went around to each room in the house and made sure the windows were closed and the blinds were down, so nobody could see us from the outside. That was our SOP (standard operating procedure)—get in, be invisible, get what you want, get out. That was one reason I didn't break into houses at night, going in always during the day. Many of the large mansions I obtained illegal access to had such large house notes that both husband and wife would have to work—one as a lawyer, the other one as a doctor possibly, sending half their income to the finance company.

During the night, with the owners in the house, the breaking and entry could potentially become an assault and robbery or even murder. One of my friends is on death row because he tried to rob a wealthy rancher in order to elope with his girlfriend. He thought he could make a quick buck, but the farmer resisted. They fought over a pistol, the pistol went off, and the farmer died. My friend ended up on death row as one of the youngest residents of this unit ever. Not my cup of tea at all. I intended to stay away from violence in any way, shape, or form. I hated to bleed.

Another reason I operated in daylight is that, if a house has been dark for a while and suddenly the lights come on, the neighbors would probably come knocking on the door asking why we were back so soon. And flashlights going from room to room would likely lead to an instant 9-1-1 call and a bunch of black and white cars parked randomly in the front and back yards.

During the day, however, none of those issues presented a problem. We had plenty of daylight to do our work and no company. The doorbell might ring. It could have been the delivery person trying to deliver an item too large for the mail slot in the door or a Jehovah's Witness or Mormon trying to coach us into their religious aberration, and we weren't interested. We were breaking the eighth commandment, and we knew it. We were not proud of it, but it was paying the bills. Emptying this house of its heavy burden would pay my bills for a while.

Since the front doors had stained glass and the windows on each side were frosted, the large open front lobby with the sweeping staircases on each side was a nice safe center place.

If I ever build a house, I would use this layout exactly. So many houses are built for inconvenience. You go shopping; come home with ten bags of groceries, and you have to struggle to get them from the back of the car in the garage to the kitchen counter and pantry. Not in this house.

The garage could have held four vehicles, but there were only three doors. The area on the far right held his lawn equipment. The left side of the garage had a counter as long as a car. You could get your groceries, drive the car into the left spot, and put all your groceries on that counter. When in the kitchen, you could just flip a switch, the wall would slide up into the ceiling and you could reach for the groceries, slide them to the kitchen side, lower the wall, and voilà. The groceries were right where they needed to be, in the kitchen, close to the pantry. This was an easy way to fill your pantry without lugging bags of groceries around corners or upstairs or through narrow corridors.

It was a beautiful home, with exclusive paneling and high ceilings. The kitchen was black marble with stainless steel appliances and a red stove with two ovens. Above the stove was a brushed stainless oval track with copper pots, spoons, and other utensils hanging from stainless steel hooks. The kitchen was immaculate! I always looked for a doggy door or pet dishes. I did not want to be bitten in the leg by a Doberman or get my ears bit off by a pit bull.

There was a large dining room with a long mahogany table and ten chairs. Around the dining room were family portraits—not photographs but real oil paintings. The largest one was the judge surrounded by his family. It looked like he had two sons and two daughters, all married, all with at least two kids. It was a large painting of a large family, all showing off their expensive oral surgery results and braces-induced, perfectly aligned, fake $4,000 smiles.

The man must have been a sports or news fanatic because there were televisions mounted in almost every room, except in this dining room. I guess he didn't want to miss any part of a show but could watch it walking from the kitchen to the dining room to the living room and never miss a beat. All the televisions were at least sixty inches wide; I was making a mental picture that, if I rolled them in blankets, I could stack them in the back of my truck with the tailgate down—and take them straight to a pawnshop! The one in the living room was slightly larger and had a slight curve to it; I was planning on taking that one home!

There was even a TV in the bathroom. I could just imagine the judge watching the news while he did a number two sitting on his gilded throne. The local vacuum service would be very busy this season. The septic tanks were filling up faster than ever, thanks to the upcoming presidential election and presidential debates being watched by everybody, including the judge making a deposit while watching them on his LCD TV in the restroom.

But that was when he was alive, and he was dead now. The TVs were dead too.

It took me a while to find all the safes. I found five of them!

Now, please understand. This was a trusted elected official, a well-known Democratic politician in a very affluent part of Houston. He ran for office successfully for many years, first as an independent attorney and then as DA and finally as county judge—always with lavish spending. He attended political dinners, held fundraisers, and rubbed elbows with the rich and famous. Having a large gold Mason ring might have had something to do with him climbing the ladder of political success so swiftly.

Well, that's enough about the house. But what was *in* his house? You would be amazed!

The safes were all different sizes, different brands, with different locks. That did not stop me, as I never used the locks. One safe was full of guns—rifles, shotguns and pistols, and boxes of bullets; you could not have added *one* more gun. His cup was running over.(I will talk about how to open safes in another chapter.)

Safe one: Guns

The first safe I found was the gun safe; it was against the wall in the library, not concealed but built into the wall. The size and color of the safe matched the interior well. It was seven feet tall and four feet wide. It took me about an hour to get access to the contents—the reason being, this safe was full of guns! Some were taller than me, and since firearms don't bend like dollar bills do, I had to make the opening in the door tall enough for the tallest one to fit through.

I am not a gun expert by far but knew that the judge had some very unusual specimens, and I kept the details of this gun cache written down somewhere, even when I sold off the guns. I had no idea of the value of these firearms, but when I learned more about them, I developed a new appreciation for the judge and his exquisite choice of investment.

Here is the list of the dozen guns I removed from his safe:

1. Cult Dragoon, 1st generation revolver, value $650,000
2. Henry, 1860, 45/70 cal rifle, $125,000
3. Luger, experimental pistol, $175,000
4. Schuetzen, 40/65 cal rifle, $650,000
5. Sharps, 54 cal rifle, $18,000
6. Volcanic, 41 cal, $28,000
7. Winchester, 1866 rifle, $38,000
8. Winchester, 1886 rifle, $12,000
9. Prussian, 71 cal, Black powder, $12,000
10. Winchester, 1873, 44/40 cal, $15,000
11. Springfield, 60 rifle, muzzle-loader, bayonet, $10,000
12. Colt, 1876, black powder, 45 center-fire $20,000

I did not know what I had there. Later, I took my time to look them up on the web and also asked one of my good friends, a gun collector, what the approximate value was. The total came up to $1.75*million*—at least in estimated value. These guns were not that easy to get rid of on the black market, at least not for that price. But still, the judge knew his weapons; that was for sure.

We carried all of the guns to the back seat of the truck, wrapping them in towels and sheets from the house, careful not to scratch them. We laid the guns carefully on the back seat; there was not enough room for all of them. The rest of the guns I had to put in the bed of the truck covered with garbage bags. The pistols filled up the floorboard behind the seats and in front of the passenger seat. I took the keys that were hanging by the alarm next to the fridge and locked the back door, and we slowly rolled to the end of the driveway. We had arrived around 8:00 a.m., and as we were driving off, I glanced at my watch. It was 4:00 p.m. Not bad for a day's work!

I sold all the guns to one man, Bobby F. He was a gun expert, and he gave me an honest breakdown—what each gun was, in great detail, including its caliber, age, and condition; how much it would be worth to an "honest" collector; how much he could get for it; and how much he could "unload" them all for. We settled on $950,000. (My first million came out of safe number one.

Crime might make you feel rich for a while if you can stand the bad taste in your mouth. It's sort of like the government spending deficit, running up the national debt. Just print money and don't worry about it. In the same way, if I gave you a hot check, you would have the feeling of prosperity for a while. That's how my life was. I had the feeling of prosperity for a while, but eventually, my house of cards came crashing down on me.

The judge's house had many beautiful oil paintings, at least one in each room and more lining the hallways. One was an original Norman Rockwell, the one where the cartoonist is painting a picture of himself. It was in a light blue frame. The painting was worth eighty grand; I removed it carefully and took it home also. I kept it in my apartment for a while, partly because I liked it so much and partly because I had a hard time finding an untraceable market for it.

Total value in safe one—$950,000.

Safe two: Gold

After looking behind most of the paintings in the house, I found one safe behind a large mural in the library. It was a painting of Tutankhamen, a famous Egyptian Pharaoh—his mask, the brilliant gold colors, the lapis lazuli were exquisite. It was almost as good as having the real mask but not as heavy. The painting was four feet wide and four feet tall. Behind it was a safe that was three feet wide and three feet tall. It was the smallest one of the four safes I cracked in the judge's house.

It took me a while to cut this one open, not because it was of superior material—there is no safe that can keep me out very long—but because of the location. It was just a little out of my reach; I had to stand on a chair. Good thing the mahogany dining room chairs were sturdy.

After I cut the door open, the brilliance of the contents superseded the brilliance of the beautiful painting covering it. The picture of Tutankhamen's gold mask was a fitting cover for the contents of this safe.

The stored wealth of this judge was most amazing; the valuable items he had stashed away in his house could pay off the deficit of a small country. I did not realize the worth of the items I found until I hauled them off in my truck to my apartment and did some research.

The safe was full of gold. There were five gold bricks, about seven by four by two inches. Each of these gold bricks weighed approximately four hundred ounces. The *Houston Chronicle* listed the current market price of gold at about $400 per ounce. That meant these bars would be worth around $160,000each. Five of these bars were worth close to $1million. The size of the bars was ideal for smuggling in the liner of your coat.

There was a box in the safe with twenty-five rolls of gold coins, forty coins in each roll. When I got home and opened them up, I found out that they were Krugerrands—twenty-five rolls of forty, totaling a thousand of them! At that time, they were worth $1,000each. There was $1million worth of gold coins in that safe. That made $2 million dollars so far, and that wasn't the whole loot.

Who wants to be a millionaire? Well, I do! And the judge had made me a millionaire, at least for a while. Who said crime doesn't pay?

Not only did I get a good education on watches and gold, but this job kept me in business for a long time. It was easy to sell the Krugerrands one at the time, and they were easy to store.

The gold bars were too much for me to handle. You can melt a ring down and take it to a pawnshop or a jeweler. But it took a formidable oven to melt down gold brick. I didn't want to cut it with a saw and lose a lot of gold dust. I decided to either try putting it in a hydraulic press or beat it flat with a hammer and sell little chunks now and then. I only took one gold bar home, but the other four I took to my favorite burial place.

Jean Lafitte had used Galveston Island years ago to bury his treasure, and I found several places on the island where I could bury them, write down the GPS coordinates, and come back for them later in life. Neither rust nor moth would bother them, as the longer I left them there, the more valuable they would become actually.

Just like with the Krugerrands, I retrieved almost all of the gold bars, but during a hasty retreat from one of my apartments, I lost the location of two bars; they are still hidden underground somewhere on the island, waiting for somebody to find them. (Treasure map in the back of the book.)

Some of the Krugerrands I buried in Galveston Island. Jean Lafitte would have been proud of me. I even drew up some treasure maps for fun. But with just the GPS coordinates, I could go back to them and have a nice start-up fund any time I needed to. And when you get out of prison with nothing, those little stashes came in handy! All I had to do is go to a pawnshop; buy a GPS device; and voilà, I was a rich man again.

The South African Krugerrand is a 22 karat, one-ounce gold coin. It also has 2.8 grams of copper alloy; used to give the coins higher durability and to make them more scratch resistant, it also gives them a unique orange-gold hue. They are still right there where I buried them, still as shiny as ever, waiting to be found.

For some of you gold diggers, here is a bit of interesting information. Somewhere on Galveston Island, there are two rolls of forty Krugerrands still buried. I wrote down the coordinates but lost them. I drew a treasure map and lost it also. I do vaguely remember what I drew. I have more of a picture memory. Still, after a particularly long and weary stay in a Texas prison, I could not remember precisely where I'd buried them. But I was consistent, used the walkways from the nine buildings, and went a certain distance from the corner and the path.

My favorite hotel to stay at on Galveston Island has always been the Commander on the Beach. (No national chain, no reservation, cash only, no record of my stay, just the way I like it.) The hotel is in the shape of an S, or perhaps more a question mark. I liked the rooms with their own little balconies and the terrific view. When I stayed there with Janet, we would often walk to the Ensalada Mexican restaurant, on the corner of 145th Street and Seawall Blvd. Janet would eat her favorite dish, pechuga de pollo. I usually had fajitas.

On our walk to the restaurant, we would pass up nine deserted houses between the seawall and Saba Ct. I buried the Krugerrands and the gold bars in the front yards of those houses. All of them had a walkway out the front door, leading to a path that ran the direction of the seawall. All of them had two palm trees, one on the left and one on the right of the path. I buried the gold bars and the Krugerrands about ten feet from the paths, in the direction of the palm trees. I wrote down the GPS coordinates and was able to find a lot of them! The coordinates where I buried the gold is in the back of the book.

With the GPS coordinates, I could walk to the exact spot and dig down and line my pockets a little bit. Without knowing the exact location, the houses are too much in the open to go there during daylight and dig up all the yards.

I tried to draw what I remembered and posted the map in the back of this book. So for you adventurous hole-digging treasure hunters who would like to find a million dollars' worth of gold, get your metal detector and little shovel out, and let me know when you find them. (I'll let you have a finder's fee.)

Day two had been relatively easy. We carried the gold bars one at a time to my truck, wrapped in towels. We put the Krugerrands in boxes and did the same. We wrapped the watches individually in paper towels, put them in plastic grocery bags, got in the truck, and drove home. We felt rich, elated, amazed! We stopped at Pappadeaux on the way home and ordered the most expensive item on the menu.

If you have the money of a judge, you might as well eat like one. We celebrated, went home, unloaded the truck, and were anxious to go back to his house and see what else the judge had in store for us. We were too wound up to watch the news. We got to bed and cuddled like spoons and fell asleep.

Total value in safe two—$1.8million.

Safe three: Cash

The other two safes were harder to find. One of them was embedded in the floor of the dining room, right in the middle under the large mahogany dining table. It was more difficult to open up, but my trustworthy Stihl grinding wheel made a nice square hole in the door.

That safe was full of money, bills this time. There was about an inch space from the top of the bills to the bottom of the inside door. I was afraid I had caused a fire, which is a disaster for a burglar. Fire alarms often are independently wired to the fire department. And those life-risking, law-abiding city workers would be right in the front yard with a big water hose pointing at you. A water gun is almost as scary as a real gun. Ask the guys that during a riot in prison; they will agree with me.

The grinding wheel cutting through this heavy metal door, threw a lot of sparks inside the safe, causing some of the bills to scorch along the edges and some of them to burn but only the top ones.

The discovery of these bills taught me a lot about the plans of the judge. There were not just American greenbacks but international currency also. There were a lot of euros. I knew many of the European countries had switched to the euro a while ago. But I had never seen one, except on TV. They were very colorful. All of them were decorated with bridges. Since my financial troubles were over for a while, they were a bridge over troubled water for me. The euros looked like monopoly money; it was hard to believe the euro was worth more than our trusty dollar. The British pounds had the queen's wiry smile on them. Those bills looked to me what money *should* look like.

But the judge was smart. In case of an American financial collapse, he could always take a pleasant, worry-free vacation to Europe. He could ride out an economic storm for a while. The judge did not have to worry about a run on the banks; he could just run to his safe. Well, not anymore. I left the house with all four safes relieved of their heavy burden, and the judge was not in a position to run at all anymore.

After stuffing the money in sacks and bringing it to my apartment, we had plenty of time to count it and stack it by nation and denomination:

- *British pounds.* Here is the breakdown of the Royal Queen's British pounds—1,500 one hundred-pound bills, 900 twenty-pound bills, and 750 ten-pound bills. Enough to buy quite a few cups of tea, I would say. Total pounds, £175,500; converted to dollars, about $219,129.
- *Euros.* All told, there were40 stacks of one hundred-euro bills, 1,000 fifty-euro bills, and 2,000 twenty-five euro bills. It looked like lots of monopoly money, as if the judge had bought the monopoly board and the bank as well. Total euros, €500,000; converted to Dollars, about $500,000.
- *US Dollars.* There were fewer American dollars than foreign currency; perhaps the judge had lost faith in our monetary system. This was not surprising, because when I tell you what was in the next safe, you will assume he had no faith in the judiciary system either. There were 1,000 Benjamin Franklins, 250 Ulysses Grants, and 2,000 Andrew Jacksons. Total dollars, $152,500.

Similar to the previous safe, the value stored in this safe was close to $1 million, this one in hard currency. The Mexican gang never found out how much money I carried out of that house; they didn't care. Because I gave the organization the full contents of the next safe, they were *very, very* happy. The gang had plenty of money, so much they had problems storing and washing it.

Not only did that keep them off my tail, it also assured me of many more tips in the future. They provided the tip. I just opened the can. They knew I was a good can opener. I guess their mafia maid never knew she was sweeping and mopping over millions every day. I wonder if the judge really needed all this money to bankroll or, perhaps, "enforce" his election campaigns every four years. Maybe he was just worried the world as he knew it would come to an end, and for him, that was true.

Or perhaps the judge had all his emergency funds ready in case he had to make a run for the border. If the news media ever found out what was in the next safe, he certainly would need pounds and euros; perhaps he should have stored some pesos also.

After opening the first three safes, I could not wait to see if there was any more and what would be in the next one. Perhaps he'd tucked away the crown jewels from the Tower of London. Maybe I would find the Star of India, stolen from the J.P. Morgan jewel collection in 1964 by Murph the Surf.

I was a thief, and I knew I was breaking the law. But the judge was an important, elected, respected official. This goes to show you, if a man is a thief, he will steal. If you make him the CEO of Enron, he will steal the whole company. Make him a Judge, and he will steal the election. Beware, Houston.

There was much more stuff in the house. He apparently was a brass collector. There were brass statues all over the house; some were life-size children. Beautiful clocks filled the house as well. Among them were two grandfather clocks, one in the entrance between the open staircase and another in the library. Some of the clocks appeared to be over a hundred years old hung in various places in the house. None of them ticked or chimed. Nobody to wind them, I guess.

We loaded up the truck and drove home with the money in pillowcases, very full and reasonably heavy. I did not have a safe in my apartment, but the door was made out of solid steel (more about that later).

Total value in safe three—$910,000.

Safe four: Cocaine

My wife and I knew that going back to the same house four times in a row was stretching it; too much traffic would arouse suspicion. But driving to the house each day in the morning and leaving each afternoon brought a sense of regularity to our trafficking. Maybe they thought the mafia maid had a daily contract to clean the house and use the back door.

We knew we were stretching it, perhaps becoming careless and forgetting our gloves. We brought food for the day and did not leave the house. We used the fridge and drank the soft drinks that were there; we took the empty cans home, trying not to leave a trail.

I had previously deducted that, in the most affluent neighborhoods, the people are very lonely. They don't know who their next-door neighbors are, whether they're healthy or sick, or whether they're wealthy or struggling. The neighbors most likely didn't even know the judge was dead. They lived alone in their big houses, entertaining themselves to boredom. In their riches, they had become poor in relationships, poor in friends, poor in *life*.

In the poor parts of town, the people were rich in relationships, rich in friends, ready to share the little they had. Talking from back porch to back porch made their camaraderie contagious.

My riches, even though temporary, did not give me a lot of friends; actually I had become more of a recluse because I kept the money laying around or just stacked in the closet. I could not open a bank account; I had become an invisible man. I would not let anybody take my picture. Later, I would find out that was why the police had such a hard time finding me; they had no idea what I looked like. Sometimes, I wanted to go back to the neighborhood where I was raised, where my dad went to work, and my mom stayed home and kept the house. She was there when we came out of school.

And on the walk back from the bus stop to the house, everybody knew who you were, looked out for you, and actually cared.

Finally, I found the fourth safe. It was in the back of the judge's walk-in closet, hidden behind the full-length mirror, very clever. The mirror had three panels; two of them folded together on the third one, revealing what I thought was a gun safe at first. But there was nothing there to shoot somebody with; instead, there was a lot of stuff to shoot *up* with.

I almost caught the carpet on fire cutting this door open. And when I had cut a hole about two by three feet and the large panel with hot, glowing edges fell in front of my feet, my sweetie and I could not believe our eyes.

In front of us were many white plastic blocks. Stacked from the floor to the top of the six-foot high safe were 150 carefully wrapped one-kilo blocks of cocaine!

I knew a doctor once who would drive to Houston, buy a kilo of cocaine for $1,000, drive back to his home in Beaumont, cut it in half, and sell half a kilo to a dealer for $1,000. Perhaps he was one of the judge's customers. But for some reason, I did not think the judge was a user *or* a dealer. Rather, I guessed he had this stashed away to buy favors from the undesirables when the occasion arose.

I left the cocaine alone; drugs are nothing but trouble.

I never did drugs and wasn't going to start now. I always felt like God (my religion came out now and then) had blessed me with a quick mind, and I did not want to lose it. I had seen plenty of guys, in and out of prison, who couldn't think straight or see straight or feel any compassion because they had wasted their brains and health with drugs. While not always visible in rotten teeth, this state can show up in rotten attitudes and bad decisions.

Total value in safe four—150 x $20,000 = $3 million according to Houston street value. But *zero* for me.

Safe five: Watches

There was a smaller safe in the bedroom upstairs. I knew the make and model; it was easy to crack open. This safe contained a lot of fine-looking watches. Up until then, I did not know much about watches. I thought the most valuable watch around was a Rolex. Was I ever so wrong.

The respectable judge was a watch connoisseur. He definitely did not buy them to wear around his wrist but as an investment. Too bad he could not take them with him where he went, but I still had two wrists, and one good watch would look just fine there. When I discovered the brand names and values, I decided a punk like me could be easily recognized as not having obtained them by an honest day of hard work. I never did wear any one of them outside my apartment—just inside, to look at how they looked. I just wanted to see the works through the glass front and back.

I also used the watches to pay my doctor in case I got sick or hurt on the job, which happened one time when the cutting blade I was using flew apart and cut the veins in my lower arms. These watches would be my "health insurance" for a while.

I looked at the names on the watches as I put them in my backpack. But I didn't recognize them. When I got back to my lair, I laid them all out. Most of them were stunningly well designed. I did some research as to their value on the web and was quite amazed. I never knew they made watches worth close to a million dollars and made only ten of them!

About the watches, that was a whole other issue. Not only did the people I dealt with have no idea what the value was, they also weren't even interested. Through my contacts with the mafia and its international connections, I was able to ship all of the watches overseas and open large bank accounts in several different branches across the city. Some of the watches I kept and wore. Some of them I continued to trade with, like trading a Patek Philippe to a doctor when I needed surgery after a burglary gone wrong.

In the bottom of the gun safe was a small electric machine. I had never seen one before, but it was a watch winder. It had room for twenty watches, and each spot was full. These were not the typical run-of-the-mill watches; there were quite a few Rolexes in the bunch. The judge was also a watch aficionado and knew how to shop for watches. I had *no* idea how exquisite or valuable they were until I did some research.

The watches I took out of the box included:

	Watch	Value
1.	Breitling Superocean	$6,100
2.	Breitling Chronomat	$6,800
3.	Breitling Deus Top Time Limited	$7,400
4.	Casio Edifice Day Date	$7,400
5.	Casio pink gold retro watch	$6,000
6.	Christophe Claret Maestro	$68,000
7.	Maurice Lacroix Auto	$5,000
8.	Meridien 19 rubies automatic	$7,200
9.	Montblanc Nicolas Rieussec	$9,200
10.	Montblanc Chronograph automatic	$5,300
11.	Omega Seamaster Planet Ocean	$6,400
12.	Oris Big Crown automatic	$7,800
13.	Panerai Luminor Marina	$6,900
14.	Patek Phillippe Geneve	$40,000
15.	Radiomir Panerai Firenze	$16,000
16.	Rolex Oyster Perpetual Datejust	$15,000
17.	Rolex Oyster Perpetual Superlative	$7,100
18.	Rolex Submariner 1,000–3,000 feet	$13,500
19.	Tissot 1853 Powermatic 80	$5,400
20.	Tissot Vintage 1853	$9,500

Total value of the watches, a little over a quarter million dollars! That would give me some nice ones to wear and a few to pay my doctor with.

Until I took those watches home and checked for the value, I had no idea that any of them were worth more than $2,000. Until then, all I ever wore were Casio solar-powered atomic watches for $89. A Rolex, until then, to me, was the status symbol of wrist wealth, but I never liked Rolexes. I had never heard of a "tourbillion."

A tourbillion is a mechanism that constantly rotates the balance wheel, balance spring and escapement of a watch, while the movement is running. It looks similar to a planet rotating in space. This is done to counter the affect of Earth's Gravity on the isochronal properties of the balance wheel and spring. The tourbillion was invented in 1795 and patented in 1801.

Nor did I know there were watch collectors all over the world who would kill for some of these watches. The total retail value for these watches was $1.5 million. By the time I had unloaded all but three, I had almost a million-dollar stashed in my penthouse safe. The judge must have not only had unlimited funds but also knowledge of what he was buying.

Watches take up very little space, and these prime pieces would only increase in value, especially when *not* worn on a wrist but kept safely and scratch-free in a temperature-controlled safe—smart guy this dead judge. Too bad, he could not wear one in his coffin; no watch battery lasts for eternity.

The judge was a man of exquisite taste in guns and watches. I had no idea of the value of those watches; I'd never heard of most of the names. I thought they would be worth about the same as a fancy Rolex and be as easy to cash in. I was very wrong. The watches were easy to carry home and conceal. I did research on all of them on the web and found all of them and their approximate value. The judge was not only a connoisseur of good guns, he was also very well informed on his choice of watches. He had a perfect inflation-free investment in both.

Some of them I kept to trade with the doctor who would do emergency surgery on me, should I get wounded one way or another. If you checked into a hospital with a bullet wound, the police *had* to be notified. I kept some of the watches as my own private health insurance. That doctor would give me as many antibiotics I wanted in trade for a watch—and help me out in the middle of the night if I needed him. He also was a watch collector, but his collection was not half as valuable as that of the dead judge.

One of the watches I kept and wore for a long time—the Christophe Claret Maestro—because it was just so unusual. Later I learned that 3 percent of the world's most expensive watches were made in Switzerland, but that they were worth *more* than the 97 percent of watches the rest of the world makes. Some of those watches, I later discovered, are made by hand. With thousands of parts, they only make *one* per year and sell for $1 million each. Some they only make fifty of, and collectors, like vultures waiting for a rotten possum, can't wait to get their hands on one.

Or when you have too many of them or when you are too lazy to move, guess what? You put your automatic watches in this expensive lazy man's watch winder, and it keeps them wound up for you. This safe had an inside light; the winder was plugged into an electric socket on the inside of the safe, and the watches were keeping perfect time. The watches slowly rotated in their cradles, just like a chicken egg rotator that ensures the eggs hatch evenly. I gathered the watches like a farmer gathered the eggs.

The value of those watches far exceeded my ability to get rid of them. You could not just walk into a pawnshop trying to pawn a ten thousand dollar watch without either the door locking behind you or your picture from the security cameras being posted around town. But one of my contacts had a friend in Europe who would send a brick of euros after he'd found out what I had. And over time, I sold all of the watches to him except one.

The value obtained from safe five was *$1 million.*

***

I didn't touch the cocaine—never did drugs, never will. I left that for my La eMe contact. We loaded our truck around 4:00p.m.

On the way home, I called my contact and told him where the key was, where to park, and how big a vehicle he needed to make one trip. He was happily surprised that his next shipment of cocaine would not have to come from somebody risking his life crossing the Mexico-Texas border but could just be picked up here in Houston at the judge's house.

Here is a recap of the loot in the judge's house:

1. Safe one (guns) netted me $950,000
2. Safe two (gold) netted me$1,800,000(hidden in Galveston)
3. Safe three (cash) netted me$910,904
4. Safe four (cocaine) netted me zero
5. Safe five (watches) netted me$256,000

    Total loot—$3,061,894

A few days of work netted me $3million. That is how I was able to buy the $1 million penthouse. One of the men I knew in the financial district scrubbed all this money clean for me, for a 10 percent fee. I gave him $500,000 for his trouble, which gave me the clear cash to run my "business." In another chapter, I'll describe the penthouse for you. I lived there for almost seven years. I really enjoyed my view. But after a home invasion and parachute escape, I sold it also and moved on (not to higher grounds).

As for now, I was rich, richer than I had ever been. But somehow, I still had an empty feeling inside. Shortly after we'd acquired the loot from the judge's house, Janet, my wife, and companion died. It all happened very quickly. She was diagnosed with acute lymphocytic leukemia. Within three months, she was gone.

I was rich but lonely and tired of running.

CHAPTER 5

ESCAPE TO THE CLEARING

Before I was married to Janet, I lived with Amanda. We lived together for two years. During that time I got her pregnant, and we had a son together. Shortly after that, she got tired of my lifestyle, and we split up. We named our son Paul; he was about four years old at the time we split. I was in the neighborhood, right off the beltway, and wanted to go see him.

Since we were never officially married, there was no divorce and no child support payments due. But I did send her money when I could. If I made a successful hit, I would send her $1,000 cash, usually in a birthday card.

She lived on the northeast side of Houston, outside Beltway 8, between Beltway 8 and Lake Houston, near Summerwood Elementary School. While I was going north on the east loop of Beltway 8, I called her and told her I was coming to see my son.

We did not part on friendly terms, and since I was not obligated to pay her child support, she usually treated me like a deadbeat dad. However, when I sent her money, she would be sweet like honey for a while. That was why I didn't politely contact her to see if it was convenient for me to spend some time with my son. I loved that little man but did not have any feelings for her anymore.

I just told her, "I'm coming over!"

She said, "No, you are not!"

I said, "Yes, I am. Be there in five." And I hung up.

Five minutes later, I turned right unto Brighton Park Drive from Bent Ridge Drive. She lived in the fifth house on the right, just passed Sun Manor Lane. It was a beautiful community with well-kept lawns—a typical, white-collar American neighborhood where $40,000 soccer mom Suburbans are parked in the driveway, while $5 worth of garage sale junk is rotting in the garage.

As I turned down her street, my "Spidey sense" was tingling. Something didn't feel right. My police scanner was quiet.

I started driving a little slower and approached her house. I was driving a Yellow Ford F-150, four-wheel drive, with a straight 6 block. I took a right turn into her driveway and sat in the truck for a few seconds, thinking. It looked like all the lights were off. But I'd just talked to her. I knew she was home a few minutes ago.

I opened the driver's side door and left it open—just in case I required a hasty retreat. I walked to the front door. There were no lights on in the lobby, but the door was cracked open. All those things made my heart pounce and my skin tingle. I knew something was really wrong. The lobby was dark, and a good thing it was. As I looked straight into the dark lobby, I could see out of both corners of my eyes, and something was moving.

Two police cruisers were pulling out of driveways about six to seven houses on each side of me.

They backed out. That was a big mistake. If they had backed in their police cars, then they could have raced toward me, but now they had to back up, hit the brake, put their transmission in forward, and accelerate from a stopped position toward me. This gave me just enough time to jump in my truck and take off.

I was blocked from both ends unless I wanted to disable a police car and trash my truck at the same time. That was not going to work. I didn't want to get caught and go to jail—again.

There was only *one* other option. I put the truck in first gear and plunged my truck between the two houses.

Most of these houses had cedar fences, held up by treated two-by-fours. The houses had been there for about ten years; so had the fences.

The treated four-by-fours you buy at your local Home Depot are *not* treated with creosote like the electric company poles; those poles might last thirty years.

These four-by-fours are usually dried and pressure treated with micronized copper azole. That's what gives them a green color. It's a poison for termites—they stay away from it—and it also prevents rotting. But in the humid Texas weather, those poles usually don't last more than ten years. While they look OK above ground, they're rotting underground. And the front bumper of my F-150 was fixing to find out if this was true or not.

The houses were about sixteen feet apart, with the fences attached to the back corner of the house. I ran over nicely laid, curved landscaping tiles and headed straight toward the spot where the two fences met.

Crash—wood splinters everywhere.

My scanner sprung to life too. In every car I drive, I install a ham radio. They are much better than CB radios. Instead of a range of one to five miles, the ham radios have a range of ten to twenty-five miles, and there is usually not much traffic. I did not have a license but used the call signs of a ham operator who had been dead a while.

I programmed all the known police and emergency vehicle frequencies in the radios. That way, I could talk when cell phones were down and hear what was going on with the blue coats. They must have suspected this and kept radio silence when I drove to my baby mama's house. But now they were talking—not just talking, hollering—and they were calling in reinforcements.

As I was crashing through the fences, I hoped and prayed there would not be any kids playing in the backyards. I had been a thief all my life but had never hurt anybody physically, even though I had hurt them financially and in several other ways.

If there were any dogs, their keen sense of hearing surely would alert them of an approaching freight train fixing to liberate them from their permanent backyard and allow them some room to roam.

I was now in the backyard of my ex-girlfriend's neighbor and took a right. From this point, instead of bulldozing through two fences meeting in the middle, I only had to flatten *one* fence to get into the next backyard.

The cops bravely tried to follow me. They did not shoot.

The truck had a lot more bottom clearance than the police cruisers, which meant they would pick up a lot more plastic yard decorations than I would.

I saw the first one slide, spin all the way around, and get stuck in the wet grass. Thanks to the differential, when one tire spins freely, the other one gives up and does not move at all. I flipped two switches in my truck; one locked the differential, and the other one put it in four-wheel drive.

They had highway tires. I had Bridgestone Desert Duelers. I had seen them on a construction truck getting seventy thousand miles heavy-duty usage and liked the pattern. I never thought they'd come in handy for an escape, trashing backyard fences in an upscale neighborhood.

I was worried about only one thing—well, two—getting away from the cops and *avoiding swimming pools at all costs.* My truck was reasonably well equipped for the task at hand, but only Jesus walked on water.

When Henry Ford designed the Model T in 1908, he was very successful in selling them to the general public. But I do not recall that anyone of them was ever used to traverse water effectively. Note to self—avoid backyards with swimming pools when you are running from the cops.

The first yard was empty, with no dogs, but there was a swing set close to the house.

Bam, I knocked down the next fence. The second police car was coming around the one that was stuck in the grass. He was in hot pursuit, and probably on his radio. I had never been able to outrun a radio with a vehicle or a helicopter with a car. My adrenaline was pumping, my thoughts were racing, my palms were sweating, and my pedal was to the metal. The furiously spinning tires were throwing large clumps of perfectly maintained backyard ten feet up in the air behind me.

That was the first fence I knocked down between backyards, but there were *nine* more to go. If my ex had lived one or two blocks over, there would have been only five or three fences; maybe I should have told her to move to a cheaper neighborhood.

The second backyard had a tree in the far right corner and a raised bed around it, I ran one tire on the raised bed on purpose; that would give me a little more lift to hit the next fence a little higher. Never knowing if there was, perhaps, a structure on the other side, I needed all the help I could get.

I made it to the third backyard—nothing there but a perfectly mown yard and a small patch of veggies, some tomato stakes. I went to the left of the tomato stakes, between them and the house—because in the fourth yard, there was a square metal storage building. I could see the roof sticking out over the fence. I didn't mind letting my Ford front bumper have a boxing match with cedar boards and pine posts, but a John Deere riding mower inside a wooden shed could have been a slight deterrent to my anxious escape.

Bang. Fourth yard—I smashed a big hole in the fence. The part that flew to the right bounced off the storage shed and flew right back at me, breaking out my passenger window. I was glad Janet was not with me. She would not have liked the little square pieces of glass in her hair. I would not have gone to see my ex if Janet were with me anyway. She knew I had no notion of going back to Amanda, but she knew I loved my son.

The next one was a chain-link fence that worried me. The 2- inch galvanized poles did not rust as fast as a two-by-four pine would. And the fencing could get hung up on the bumper or somewhere underneath my truck. But going back was really not an option.

The road and, consequently, the backyards were slightly curved to the right. I had lost sight of the cops. If they were smart, they would have just backed up and taken the clean smooth concrete of Brighton Park Drive. But there were only two cars so far, and one was stuck. I was hoping the other one was a wannabe Texas cowboy who intended to brag to his buddies, "Yeah, I took that police cruiser through all them backyards and caught that filthy crook."

Later I found out I lost him at this chain-link fence; his cruiser got tangled in it.

Bang, ching. Yard number five. I decided to run over a galvanized post right in the middle of my bumper. It was a good choice; when the post bent or snapped, the fence went down with it. If I had tried to break through between two posts, it would have required twice as much power, and the chain link might have acted like a slingshot, throwing me back into the previous fence. Both my front and rear tires rolled over with no problem.

Bang, crash. For yard number six, I had to veer to the left. This house came further into the backyard, leaving only about two feet on each side of my truck. I did not have a choice; I had to hit it here. When I crashed through that fence, my truck shot about three feet up into the air. They had one of those fancy stainless steel barbeque pits parked right against the fence; it caused me to fly up and come down hard.

I almost lost control and thought about crashing to the left and getting back on the road, but I was afraid that Smokey the bear would be waiting for me there. So I continued my backyard cruising, the engine roaring.

I saw another cedar fence ahead of me, this one covered in a sweet potato vine, beautiful, large heart-shaped leaves, bright green. Sorry to destroy your meticulously grown vine, neighbor. The fence folded under me. Some of the vines were stuck on my right mirror; they were actually quite pretty the way the sun was hitting them.

Bang, *crash*—yard number seven. This house had a veranda slightly built in and recessed in the middle of the house. An elderly couple was enjoying their afternoon iced tea and snacks. When I came roaring through their backyard, knocking the first fence down, I raced past them and waved, before taking out their fence on the other end of the yard. They dropped their iced tea glasses on their glass table, breaking both the glasses *and* the table. Perhaps their insurance would pay for the glasses, the fence, *and* the table; I was hoping. My mind was racing faster than my truck.

Bang. Yard number eight had beach balls, lawnmowers, rakes, and bicycles; there was more trash in this yard than Carter has pills. Don't people realize you need to keep your yard properly maintained and picked up in case a fool like me takes your fences down on both sides and decides to use your backyard as an obstacle course? I hit a plastic basketball court head-on. The backboard, the hoop, and the net broke off and landed in the back of my truck. I saw it there later when I abandoned my truck. After this kind of abuse, the truck would be too damaged to be used as a trade-in. It did not belong to me anyway; it was hot, with false plates, part of my SOP on vehicle maintenance (more of that later).

After swerving through the obstacle course of plastic toys, destroying a few basketballs and beach balls in the process, I was ready for the next yard. All during this chase, my ham radio never stopped giving me updates on the black-and-whites chasing me.

Bang, another cedar fence hit the deck. Yard number nine almost did me in. The south side of the house was built very far into the backyard; there was barely enough room for my truck. I had to drive so close to the fence on the left that I slapped my mirror on the poles holding the cedar fence. I had to go around a tree and squeeze my truck between the house and the fence. My right mirror hit the corner of the house, shattering it. Luckily for me, the passageway was narrow, but the fence was weaker than either of the previous ones and flew into the air when my bumper hit it.

Squash. I was now in yard number ten and could see a street—Summerwood Lakes Drive. Thankfully, this kind homeowner did not want a fence between him and the road. He wanted to make sure everybody who drove by could see he was planning to win yard of the month. After I roared through his immaculate front lawn, his chance of getting that purple ribbon and yard sign would be postponed quite a bit. I ripped two large muddy trenches, throwing sods with my four tires ten feet into the air and topsoil from my rear axle even further back than that. His yard now looked to me as if some early-bird farmers had taken their tractor and milk jugs through it to milk the Holsteins.

I was back on the road, and I really needed some concrete to sling the mud off my tires. But it was not to be. I turned right on Summerwood Lakes Drive. That road ends in a "T" at Sand Mountain Lane. A police car with lights flashing was turning unto my road, headed straight toward me.

I knew he was coming. He'd announced his presence and direction of approach to his buddies, and I was privileged to that information also. There were more cars headed in my direction.

If you wonder why there are so many on the police payroll, now you know; it takes at least three cops in cruisers to catch one criminal in a pickup truck. Well, at least they were hopeful and trying very hard. I was thinking harder but figured, *Hey, I was able to shake the first two cops dragging them behind me popping cedar board fences as fast as you can say, nail them. Perhaps I can use that same modus operandi and lose some more.*

I took a right into a front yard between Sky Brook Lane and Caney Springs Lane. My backyard escapades were not over yet. I had twelve yards, I mean *back yards*, to go and three swimming pools. They almost did me in—sure raised my blood pressure.

The first yard went OK. I kept knocking down fences—four-wheel drive, differential locked—like a bull in the china cabinet.

No fence left behind. The second yard was narrower; it caused me to swerve and regain control. My mind was racing, the engine was roaring, and my ham radio was very busy relaying useful information.

The third yard had a pool, quite a surprise when you're laying down a cedar fence, and it becomes the runway for you to dive your truck straight into an oval pool.

Luckily, pools usually have a lot of cement around them, lest the tender feet of the owners get grass between their toes or the dripping chlorine kills the vegetation. My left tire was on the tile edge of the pool, two inches from the water. The widest flat part was first. It took me by surprise; I swerved and bounced to the right and made a slight arch around the pool.

Bang. Another fence. I'd lost count now. The next five yards were just *bang, bang, bang.* "Thank you, ma'am, for access to your backyard. Be seeing you now. Have a nice day. Y'all come back, ya hear."

Bang. There were *two* pools, one at the house on my left, whose yard I was ripping up beyond recognition and one on the other side of the four-foot chain-link fence. I guess they liked to share pool toys or perhaps had a swimming suit contest going. Or maybe they jumped over the fence into the neighbor's pool to see if the water was bluer on the other side. I don't know. But it was scary for a Ford F-150 to again have to take the middle road. I knocked over a dozen galvanized posts. I was no longer worried about what was happening to the fence. I had done thousands of dollars of damage in five minutes and scared a lot of people, including myself. Oh, I forgot to tell you that I had a rock climbing plate mounted to the bumper; it continued under the engine and extended past the front axle. This had protected my oil pan from puncturing and the truck suffering a quick demise through loss of oil.

The pool on the right was in the yard of the last house on the cul-de-sac. There were no more houses behind that one but, instead, a field. Since I was already straddling the fence with my truck, I could either go through four more yards or hit the empty field. I choose the road of least resistance; my truck had dealt with enough resistance already.

At the end of the field was a dirt road. I roared towards it. I took a hard left turn and drifted a lot, throwing rocks and sand up in the air behind me like an Oklahoma dust storm. Why, do you wonder, did I take another left? Because that was the direction that the previous policeman had come from.

As an escape artist and runner, you learn they usually do not come from the same direction twice. Another police car would be approaching me from the right I assumed. My scanner had already informed me of his not-so-gentle approach and that more black-and-whites would be joining the party soon. They were figuring out what roads to block and where to lay the spiked strip. A helicopter was en route also.

All the various inputs made me decide a left turn would give me the greatest advantage of escape. I raced toward Sand Mountain Lane and took a swift right. Sand Mountain Lane makes a gradual turn to the right passing a cul-de-sac on the right. Right past the cul-de-sac on the right was a short street. It was a dead end, but with a four-wheel drive, there are not very many dead-ends I'd just discovered. There was a deep drainage ditch with four feet of water. I turned right, lost control, and rolled over once.

Rolling down the ditch, my right side came up. Then my wheels came up. I was hanging upside down for a second, and the truck kept going until it made a complete roll. The truck was right side up now. But in four feet of water, my feet were getting wet, and the water kept rising. I sat there for a few seconds. I could see the flashing lights of police cars flying passed me. They did not see the short dead-end street I'd taken but, instead, kept racing down Sand Mountain Lane, which turned in to Hawkins Bend. They took Hawkins Bend all the way down to the end and took a right turn on Graham Springs Lane.

The engine had died, but the contact was still on. And on my scanner, I could hear that the police were pretty sure they were right on my tail and would have me in custody shortly. They were wrong.

They'd missed me; they couldn't see me. Because the ditch was just deep enough, the top of my truck wasn't visible if you were sitting in a car on Sand Mountain Lane. If you were standing up, perhaps you could have seen the top of my truck. Four, five police car, sirens going, lights flashing, raced passed me, oblivious to my exact location.

I knew I didn't have much time.

I unbuckled and left my phone on the seat in the water; it was destroyed anyway. Plus, my ex would have given them my phone number, and they could easily trace it and triangulate my location. For that reason, I never kept a phone very long. I climbed out of my truck, crossed the drainage ditch, climbed up on the other side, and started running through the woods as fast as I could. This was an undeveloped area with pine trees and yaupon. The pine trees were about thirty feet tall and about two feet thick. The yaupon was five or six feet high and very hard to get through.

Yaupon is the Texas white-tailed deer's favorite food. How those bucks could make their way through the yaupon with their big racks always puzzled me.

I was still going south, trying to put as much distance between me, my truck, and my ex's house as quickly as possible. I knew that, eventually, those highly trained officers would find out they were chasing their own tail and had lost mine.

It would just be a matter of time before they would find my truck. Seeing that a helicopter would not have helped them locating me unless they had infrared heat cameras (they were not installed on all of the choppers yet), most likely, they would bring the dogs. Enough of my scent was left in the truck to give their pets a good whiff of me. Their olfactory senses would make them drool most likely. These dogs were ready to take a bite out of crime, but I was not prepared to be bitten. I had been chased by dogs once before.

And it was a terrifying experience—just imagine barks and howling and panting, slobbering mouths and growling teeth getting closer and closer to your tender flesh.

I ran as fast as I could. It was like running through a gauntlet; the bushes were hurting me on both sides.

I knew the cops were drooling too. I'd just wrecked about twenty yards, and they'd failed miserably to serve and protect the backyard ornaments of their taxpayers.

I ran with my arms in front of my face as fast as the shrubbery would let me. My clothes began to tear off my body. The sharp edges of the yaupon made shredded wheat out of my shirt and my undershirt. Good thing I was wearing Carhartt shorts; they're practically bulletproof; otherwise, it would have torn off my shorts and my tighty-whities. I felt like Sir Henry Morton Stanley chopping his way through the African jungle looking for David Livingston. Except I did not have a machete; I used my hands and elbows. They started to bleed as the pointy branches tore into my flesh.

In some places, there were narrow paths that looked like deer tracks. But I think they were four-wheeler trails made by the park rangers who maintained this piece of pristine wilderness. I kept heading south, directly away from the neighborhood where the angry cops were chasing me now. I pushed and pushed through. I saw a faint clearing up ahead. When I arrived there, I found a dirt lot with a small cabin in the middle.

It looked like a log cabin model home, built somewhere else and placed here by the properly owner as a home away from home or, possibly, shelter in the time of storm. It was unusually quiet, almost tranquil in this spot. You couldn't hear any highway noise—no sirens, no voices, and no car alarms. I dropped my scratched-up arms down my body and circled the cabin. There was an oak front door with no window. The other windows were small; it was a two-story cabin, about thirty-by-thirty feet square.

It appeared that, in the past, this spot had been a clearing for a drilling rig or perhaps a work over rig from an oil well drilled a long time ago. And after it was no longer profitable, the driller had removed the pump jack and all the other drilling equipment and eventually moved this cabin onto the clearing. The white crushed rock prevented the grass from encroaching on the cabin. Along the edge of the lot, I found a tire iron, normally used to mount or dismount a twenty-two-inch tire from a wheel on the rig haulers. If you had a flat in the oilfield, you were too far away from a tire shop to have your flat fixed, so you had to do it yourself. Most of the roughnecks had enough muscles and guts to bust that tire off the wheel with a sledgehammer, tire tool, and some grease.

After the tube was patched, they used the same grease or soap and the sledgehammer to beat the tire back on the rim. A tire tool was round, about as thick as your thumb, with a flat but not very sharp edge on one end. I used that tire tool to pry the front door open without doing too much damage. Nobody home.

I quickly went through the house and found a drawer in the kitchen with lots of junk—screws, batteries, pencils, and so on. (Doesn't every house have one of those?) I found a small hammer and some nails. Then I went to the front door and nailed it shut with five nails. Afterward, I went upstairs and hid under the bed. It was kind of foolish. I should have just lay on the bed. If they'd have found me inside the house, hiding under the bed was amateurish. But I was tired, worried, hungry, and sweating.

It is at those times that you worry about whether crime pays. It doesn't. And I hadn't even committed a crime. I'd just wanted to see my son. That wasn't a crime; there was no restraining order against me. But my ex-girlfriend knew I was on the Houston Most Wanted list, and she was like a Judas. If she could make money turning me in, she would; she tried and almost succeeded.

I lay there under the bed, waiting. And what I'd prophesied in my mind would happen happened. I heard the long wailing howl of K9s, first faintly and then louder and louder.

About fifteen minutes later, they were circling the house—not mice and men but dogs and men. I don't know how many. There were no lights on in the cabin, and the door was locked shut, and I was not stupid enough to stick my head through the curtains, hollering, "Surprise!"

They also did not say, "Come out, come out from wherever you are." But they wanted to.

I heard men talking, cars drive up, men arguing, and banging on the door and all the windows. The big bad wolf in cop's clothing was huffing and puffing, wanting to blow my house down. But they could not. Later, I found out why.

They did not have a search warrant!

I felt sorry for them. I did not have permission to enter the house, but I had anyway. It was almost sad that I could get away with breaking and entering, and they could *not*. The same law that I'd broken protected me now—how ironic. They couldn't get to me because they didn't have a little piece of paper that said they could.

Next, the dogs were loaded in their cages inside vehicles; they were barking less. Then I heard the men drive off, and the barking faded into the distance, just as they'd gotten louder when they'd come to the house. I was relieved. Nobody had come into the house. I lay under the bed, still a little worried but amazed.

The voices were lower, and fewer. Several more cars drove off. Then there were just two men left and two police cars, I could see the faint red and blue and white flashes through the sheer of the bedroom windows bounce off the walls to my hiding place under the bed. Then they quit talking. I never could understand what they were saying. The walls were too thick, and the double windows made the cabin a quiet place.

The last two men got in their cars and drove off. I was alone again, naturally. But I knew that this would not be a long-term situation. They might be calling a judge right now and obtaining a search warrant for this property posthaste. I took a shower. After washing my arms off, the wounds did not look too bad. I had a lot of scratches, but most were skin deep—no cuts like a knife would make.

I rummaged through the house. There was a walk-in closet full of nice men's clothes, exactly my size. I tried on different pants and shirts. I settled for black cargo pants and a redshirt. It was not very cold at night, perhaps in the sixties. The coat I took was stonewashed blue denim with a sheep-looking liner and collar. It had many pockets. I liked that, even though I had nothing to put in them.

I pulled the nails out of the front door, exited the cabin, and nailed it shut from the outside, this time with just one nail way at the top of the door. I wiped the fingerprints off the hammer, tossed it in the woods, and started walking south again. This time, I slowly and carefully avoided the yaupon. Eventually, I came to a dirt road and heard a train in the distance. I walked about a mile to the railroad tracks. I sat there and waited until a slow train came by, heading southwest. I was familiar with the tracks coming in and out of Houston from several directions. If you're a runner like I was, you have to know that any road can be an escape road, just as you learn in the prison that everything can be a weapon.

I took the train downtown and called a friend of mine from a washateria / dry cleaner. He came and picked me up and dropped me off at my house. My wife had been worried; she hadn't heard from me almost all day.

I told her my story. She cleaned my cuts and bruises with peroxide and put triple antibiotic salve on it. Then we made love. I held her until we fell asleep. It is good to have somebody who cares for you, especially when the whole world chases you.

CHAPTER 6

THE GOLDEN KEY

The police pulled us over, my nephew Fred and me. We had garbage bags full of parcels on the back seat. I told my nephew to deny everything. We had letters, magazines, and many parcels with us, illegally obtained from drop boxes. When the cop searched the car and found all that stuff, he became very suspicious. He arrested both of us, put us in handcuffs, and took us to the police station. There, he put us in a room and emptied the garbage bags with parcels on long white tables. I lied and told him the car didn't belong to me; it was a friend's car, and we had no idea how the bag full of parcels had gotten there. The car was stolen. I had bought it at the traveling parking lot.

He called the Inspection Service. You think I got in big trouble over this?

Let me take you back to the beginning.

As a criminal, I was careful to choose my line of work, my targets, or my specialty. Like I said before, I did not shoot or harm people in any way physically—or perhaps I should say bodily. But I did rob people. I had become an expert thief.

I robbed stores, houses, and parcel delivery services. If you're thinking about going into this line of work, I strongly suggest you do *not* rob the latter. For one, they have units in many states, and consequently, you will get the FBI on your tail. They have a nationwide expert crime-fighting force with a big budget and lots of toys at their disposal. Compare this to the hick town sheriff offices that have to get on the phone and beg their constituents for money to buy their duty weapons.

The other reason is there is no money in parcel delivery businesses. Just do the math. If a parcel delivery businesses has six counters, the company probably employ three workers during the day helping customers. They are severely understaffed and have had more and more budget trouble because of the email and internet and their friendly competitors. If there are three clerks at the window, they close out at night and leave $100 cash to start out the next day. And their stock drawers hold about the same amount. Four hundred dollars is not enough to spend time in a federal prison or "Club Fed" over. Note to self—Avoid robbing parcel delivery businesses; it is not worth the trouble. Most people pay with debit cards. There isn't much cash there.

But I guess I was hardheaded and stupid enough to do this half a dozen times. That was probably because they were such easy targets; their alarm systems sucked. And maybe it also had something to do with there being one on every street corner, sometimes dark street corners.

It seemed like, if every other business closed in a particular part of town because of the economic depression, the local delivery service, or mail room as some are called, would not move. It amazed me how many parcel delivery businesses had empty lots beside it and empty business across the street from it. No streetlights, no police controls, simple alarm systems. I visited the local parcel delivery businesses several times to relieve them of their heavy burden. To my surprise, one little thing I picked up at one of my nightly visits at a business like that kept me floating in checkbooks, driver licenses, checks to cash, debit, and credit cards for over a year.

This is how I went about robbing this joint.

I would do business at a target office, standing in line at the busiest time of day. These companies' goal was to have their wait time in line be less than five minutes, but it was usually closer to ten. As I mentioned earlier, there is a chronic nationwide lack of staffing, which meant overworked supervisors and insufficient staffing scheduling. In those ten minutes, I would observe everything going on there.

I saw where the people stood, where their money went, where they walked, who was the lead salesperson, where their change drawer was, and where their stock was. It was apparent they didn't have enough supplies in their own drawers; they constantly had to add from the main stock. Sometimes, they had to get it out of the main safe. That was my target—the location of that safe, where the bulk of the money and valuables were kept.

I'd observe how close to the windows it, how close to the door, and whether there a line of sight from the outside; usually, there was not. The individual safes were plain, very old, very well made, and hard to open. And when I made a sufficiently large hole in the door, there were drawers you couldn't slide out for lack of room. I did not take the door off, I cut a hole for access. But *if* there was a walk-in safe, my ears pricked up.

A lot of convenience stores had large floor-to-ceiling windows all along the street side, which means, during a break-in, you would be visible to any customer driving or walking by. Not so at parcel delivery businesses. Usually, there were large windows on each side of the front doors. There were smaller windows higher up in the box for rent section and in the lobby. I was scouting my entrance and exit ways for approach during the night.

I might do this several times, drawing a map in my small moleskin agenda while I was in line, as my mentor Hank had taught me. While acting like I was updating my agenda, I was making a floor plan of the site. I would take meticulous notes, sometimes going home and drawing it into AutoCAD. I would mark the walls and the safes in different colors, making sure the doors and windows were allocated the appropriate space and location. I would draw dotted lines of my entrance, mark the spot where I would spend most of my time gaining access to the safe, and make another dotted line in a different color planning my exit.

The exit path was more important for a burglar for two reasons. You might have to get out very quickly when it was clear a lawman was on the way. The other reason was, if you picked up a pretty good haul and you had to make several trips back to your vehicle in which to bring the loot home, you had to have a clear path, not through a window seven feet up in the air. Preferably, your escape would be through a fire exit door. They were *not* supposed to be locked according to OSHA. Even though OSHA rules didn't apply to them for a long time, I rarely would find a fire exit locked. *If* you were inside, you could push down the bar, after disabling the alarm; open the door; and keep it blocked open with a pencil, a ruler, or a chair, just about anything that was lying around.

Later that same day, right after dark, after their closing time, of course, when the last supervisor had left and locked the doors, then it was time to start my shift. I would begin by cutting the main phone lines coming into the building. They were usually easy to find. Ma Bell had the same gray plastic boxes mounted on the back of every building in town, including your house. The box was usually sealed with a small, hard plastic seal with a steel wire going through an oval clip on the box. I snapped the seal. I opened the gray box where all the phone lines came into the building and clipped them all off.

Then I would walk about a hundred yards away and wait. Some alarm systems send a signal to a central security office if the phone connection is lost. With parcel delivery businesses and their slow grinding gears, that was usually *not* the case. If there was no police presence in fifteen minutes, I would walk back to the building and force entry, sometimes by picking the lock, sometimes by using a crowbar. I wanted that done quickly, as it was the most public and visible and, sometimes, noisy part of the job. Vehicles driving by or joggers or people walking their dog would be able to observe that I was *not* the guy with the right set of keys, just by the motions I was making.

This had to be done swiftly and efficiently, making sure the damage to the door wasn't visible from the outside and that I could lock the door behind me. I didn't want somebody to walk in behind me and tap me on the shoulder, saying, "Surprise!"

This delivery service office was older; it had steel doors but flimsy doorjambs and framing. Instead of the door breaking, the wall dented back where the bolt entered, and the door flew open, knocking the crowbar out of my hands. It made a clinking noise when it fell on the cement walkway. The sound of the crowbar hitting the ground was something I desperately wanted to avoid. Quiet as a mouse did not fit this break-in anymore.

I grabbed the crowbar, stepped into the office, and closed the door behind me. There was a deadbolt lever that did not need a key from the inside to lock it. This allowed me to break open the door, get in, close it behind me, and lock it. Unless another thief had a crowbar with the same schedule that night or the supervisor came back to pick up something he forgot, I was going to be alone all night.

One time when I had gained illegal entry into an office, somebody did come in after me. It was a terrifying experience. I hid under the desk quickly. He turned on the lights, walked right passed me, picked up his cell phone from the desk, turned off the lights, left, and locked the door. He never saw me or my backpack leaning against the desk or my Stihl two-cycle gas engine grinder. You would think the orange and white disk grinder sitting in front of the drab green safe would be a tell-all, but he never saw it. People are so busy with their own lives; they only look to their own thing, never to the things of others. Apparently, he'd left his cell phone on his desk, gotten home, and missed it badly enough to come back for it.

The walk-in safe that I'd scouted out and targeted for content removal was in a perfect location. If you were a customer standing in line or in front of the counter, you could not see it. Therefore, it was not visible through any of the windows near the front door. People could come in twenty-four hours and get their mail out of the for-rent boxes, which was somewhat of a concern to me. The grinder was noisy, the sparks looked like a firework's sparkler, and the smoke sometimes appeared similar to when you leave your bagel in the toaster too long.

But it was after 10:00p.m.; usually, people do not leave their house that late to pick up a bill they don't have the money to pay for. I was alone, ready to go to work.

I cranked up the Stihl gas-powered grinder. It had a sixteen-inch wheel. I previously had experimented with different-size grinding/cutting wheels. Mine had a B80 diamond wheel premium grade sixteen-inch wheel, and I had a spare wheel with me. One time during a safe-cutting job, the wheel broke, and a piece flew off and cut my arm right below the elbow. It bled profusely. I left everything there and went to a doctor friend of mine, who stitched me up—no questions asked. I paid him with a watch. That was at a pawnshop. More of that in another chapter.

It would have been a little faster if I knew the combination of the safe, but I had all night. Every bank and every safe can be broken into; it's just a matter of time. The bigger, stronger, and sturdier the safe is constructed, the more time you have to catch me in the act and the more time it took for me to gain access. But every safe is just a time delay for theft.

Just recently, some guys broke into a bank in England, emptying the safe-deposit boxes of unsuspected rich people. You know how they did it? Time! They spent all weekend at that location, planned it, broke through a thick concrete wall, pried the boxes open one at a time, and went home a lot richer. I studied my profession, giving scores to guys who got away or not; this one was an A+. They pulled off a smooth heist and got away with it, for a while at least.

A lot of safes of similar age and model have three layers of steel—a thin outer layer; below that one, a harder, almost cast-iron alloy steel; and then a space for the gears that push the retaining pins to the left and right into the sides of the safe. (That's why it's never a good deal to try to remove the door.) The next layer of steel is a much a softer blend of metals. The newer safes have a glass plate in the door also. If you break that glass, it jams everything, and you might as well go home.

In prison, I took a free locksmith course offered to anybody in the nation who wants to improve their lifestyle and change their career by becoming a successful, highly paid locksmith. There was a catalog with a selection of books you could order with detailed instructions, diagrams, blueprints, and cutaway of locks. But also, to my surprise, there was one book on safe construction. Talk about making good use of my prison time—I studied my profession and gained quite a bit of knowledge about safes and locks.

I learned a lot from that, including the history of safe design and construction. I learned why certain metals were used and where and how the internal cams interlocked with each other. The course taught you why a combination lock had to be turned left, right, left, and stopped at a certain point. I was stunned when I was in my cell at a federal prison and opened my mail, and in there was an envelope with a book on safe construction. And I was locked up in that prison for safe deconstruction. Perhaps it was part of my successful rehabilitation into society.

Yes, dear taxpayer, I used my time being locked up to, let's say, "better" myself. How they ever allowed the locksmith course through the prison mailroom scrutiny is beyond me. At least you can say that I made good use of your taxpayer money to provide me food and lodging in the prison system. I learned a lot. I became a better locksmith, which came in handy during lock picking.

Most vaults in banks are made when the bank building is constructed. They plan the location and the protection of the safe first and design the building around it. They plan the thickness and type of cement and the strength of the rebar to prevent a break-in from the bottom, top, and three sides. The door that is usually the weak spot is often afoot thick also. The walls are thick reinforced concrete. When the bottom, top, and sides are hardened and set, the door is installed. It's usually made of stainless steel with concrete in between. Then they finish the bank building around it.

The New York federal reserve vault is deep below the streets of Manhattan. This massive gold depository is considered such an impenetrable vault that it stores more US gold than Fort Knox. The underground location of that vault makes it particularly hard to approach. Fort Knox, as the name implies, would have a lot of high-powered rifles with scopes and very committed guys pointing them at you if you tried to rob that one.

Not so at the local parcel delivery office. Everything was *on* the floor, not below it, and there were no armed guards. A lot of the safes there were not built into the wall but had large iron casters and could be rolled around—by a strong person, that is. And they were not worth tearing into, as there was nothing much of value there.

This safe was exactly as some of the manuals described it. The ins and outs of the locking mechanism did not interest me, I was cutting it to pieces, but my knowledge of the metallurgy used in the construction of this safe could significantly contribute to my prompt access to the contents.

The diamond wheel was not a good choice on the final layer; it would get clogged up and bogged down by the soft aluminum particles embedded in the steel. The metal the inside of the door was made out of had a diamond sparkle look.

That is why I also carried the abrasive wheel. It was suitable for cutting asphalt and softer materials. It wouldn't get clogged up like the diamond wheel; it would just wear away and turn the outer edge into dust, revealing a new layer.

Banks are in business to protect your stuff. That's why they spend a lot of money on a variety of security systems. Not only do they build a very large, impenetrable safe, but they also invest in laser trip wires, motion detectors, and decibel sensors and CCTV video cameras. Cameras have now evolved to be so small they can be hidden practically anywhere.

It was a good thing this company had not invested in a decibel sensor, as it would have gone off this instant and called in the law. I had the muffler of my Stihl cutter modified by an expert mechanic. He fixed mopeds and small motorcycles. Some kids like the muffler loud, and often the parents like the muffler quiet. He could make it go either way. I had taken the Stihl to him and asked him to make it as quiet as possible, and he did. I believe he inserted steel wool in between the baffles. He made holes where there weren't any and closed off holes he deemed to be the noisiest.

My turn. I cranked up my professional cutoff machine. Usually, these are used in construction sites to cut rebar sticking out of concrete. It eats up steel like a hot knife through butter. A simple one-inch bar would be cut smooth in half in about thirty seconds; my job was a little harder and would take a little more time.

I marked an outline on the door of the safe with white chalk. This was my cutting target—a rectangle, one foot wide, two feet high, and about two feet off the ground. I made the hole just big enough for my skinny rear end to go through.

I started cutting, first the top cut about shoulder high. The sparks flew to my right, hitting a carpeted wall. That worried me a bit, but it did not catch fire; the iron sparks were cold by the time they hit the wall. The blade did its job well, penetrating the top layer of steel of the safe in a smooth, straight line; I cut it all the way from the left top mark, across the top, dragging the Stihl toward me.

I proceeded to start the cut on the right. I could tell from previous jobs this was a cheaply constructed safe. That's what you get when you go with the lowest bidder. The outer steel was about a quarter-inch thick; this door was not reinforced with concrete but had Teflon on the inside—the same material used in bulletproof vests. What did they think? That I was going to use a cannon to shoot through the door? But it was messy, dusty, and nasty. I put on a mask—the same kind people who have allergies or colds wear over their noses and mouths, simple paper with two elastics behind your ears.

I kept cutting. The blade moved slowly downward, following the white mark, toward the bottom corner. The sparks hit the floor and bounced back up at me. My Carhartt pants protected me from sparks and burns; they are as tough as they say they are. I was at the bottom right corner now. I turned the saw off and took a break.

I stopped and listened, for anything—people, cars, unusual sounds. It was eerie silent. Nothing! I walked around the building a little bit, staying away from any location where I was visible from the outside. There was a small break room close to the safe, I opened the fridge and helped myself to a cold Mars bar. I could use the calories, as that saw was heavy.

I was alone—just me the saw and the safe ready to release its contents to me any minute now. I started to get as excited as little Jimmy on Christmas morning, ready to open his gifts.

The next cut I made was the bottom cut; that way, the last cut would be the left one, and the plate that I cut would swing like a door.

If I made the bottom cut last, not only would the weight of the door be on my blade pinching it, but also, when the cut was finished, it would fall toward me, scraping my legs and hitting my toes. It happened once; that was why I'd changed my cutting pattern.

The bottom cut was short. It didn't take me very long. I didn't hit any unforeseen objects or obstacles, and everything went smoothly.

For the last cut, I lifted the saw up, pushed the gas to max rpm, and started cutting at the left top mark. I was careful to connect to the top cut, so as not to end up with hanging chards—or, more properly, a hundred-pound hanging hot piece of steel that was swinging like an autumn leaf on a tree, me not knowing when and at which direction it was going to drop. I wanted control of the situation. I carefully moved the spinning blade down to meet the other corner.

There is no use in pushing or exerting too much energy on the blade. You have to let the tool do the work. If you don't push at all, it will just polish the outside. If you push too much, the saw bogs down, and the rotation speed will be such that no cut is made. The diamond blade was doing just what it was made for, slipping through the steel like a wooden boat through the surf. But instead of creating a spray of water, I was creating a shower of sparks. Good thing the floor was vinyl; any carpet would have started smoldering by now. Where the mainstream of sparks was hitting the tiles, they were discoloring, turning brown and then black. I needed to hurry up.

Almost at the bottom, the last inch, I backed up a little on the saw, not sure if the plate would fall out or not. *Clink*, the piece was loose. But it sat in the door and would not fall out. I carried a small crowbar in my backpack, and with a little prying and persuasion, the one-by-two-foot hot steel plate fell on the ground in front of the door; I shoved it to the right. It would not slide well because the blade actually melts the steel on contact and leaves irregular shaped molten edges.

I could see inside the safe now. I used my small LED flashlight, which I was careful not to use except pointing it inside the safe. The flashlight had a deep inset lens that could be adjusted to beam or spot but not be visible from the side. There was a red light switch on the outside wall to the left of the safe. I flipped it up. A light came on in the safe; the exposed 75-watt bulb was mounted on the wall toward the back of the safe and did not shine any considerable lumens worth through the hole I cut. I grabbed my backpack and carefully, deliberately stepped inside the safe.

On my right were gray cabinets with steel drawers. All the drawers had little white tags; those were the specialty items. I did not care about them. I opened the drawers, but closed them quickly. I was looking for items that were easy to carry in bulk and easy to dispose of. I stuffed my backpack full dollar bills—ones, fives, tens, twenties, and one hundreds.

On a nail, attached to the wall was an old brass key; it looked odd to me, vintage-like. I took the key and stuck it in my back pocket with my wallet, forgetting about it instantly; it had no apparent value, just looked old. First, I lowered the backpack through the hole; it barely fit. Then I carefully stepped out of the safe. Since my pockets were bulging, I had to manipulate a little to step through the one-by-two-foot hole.

My work was done. I left a mess, picked up my saw, made my way toward the door, opened it slightly, and looked out. Nothing there. I casually walked around the building, looking inside like an ordinary passerby would. Then I walked a few blocks to my truck and drove home.

When I got home, I showed Janet my haul. She was excited. We kissed; she made supper; and after we ate, we stored all the money in a box below the clothes behind the shoes in the walk-in closet.

When I took my clothes off to go to sleep, I found that brass key in my back pocket and lay it on the nightstand. When I lay in bed, I grabbed that key, spun it around in my hands for a while, looked at it really closely, and wondered what it was for. And why did it have to have the protection of the safe? I laid it back down and kept wondering what significance it had.

I held Janet until she went to sleep. When she snored lightly, I slowly let her go and turned back around to the nightstand. I picked up that mysterious-looking key again, turning it over and over in my hand. Holding it up close, I saw it had folded patterns, cutouts on both sides, larger and thicker than a house key and longer too; and it was made out of brass. All these anomalies puzzled me. What is it for? And why was it in the safe?

A few days later, I was stopped at a red light. It stayed red a long time. I looked around to see if I had been followed. On the right corner of that street, below the traffic light was a drop-off box. There was a delivery business driver in front of one of the metal drop-off boxes. It was one of those places where people can drop of packages without going to the brick-and-mortar building. He inserted a brass key, which was attached to his belt, in the lock of that big box. The door opened up toward him, and he proceeded to take hands full of packages out of that big box and put them in his delivery van.

A light went off in my mind. Could mine be the same brass key?

The light turned green. I drove to the next light, took a right, and took another right at the next corner and another right two blocks down. I was back on the same road where I'd seen the man empty the drop-off box. One block farther down, on the corner where that drop-off box was, there was an Exxon Mobil. It was a bustling station with about eight gas pumps. There was much traffic—people running in and out to pay for their gas; snacks; or a *Houston Chronicle*, my favorite paper, of course.

Nobody noticed me parking my car close to the blue box, getting out, inserting that steel key in the half-inch round hole, and turning it.

Wow! It worked. The door opened, and I had access to the drop-off box. I was amazed, shocked, excited, and scared at the same time. My thoughts raced. I thought of all the possibilities. People mailed almost anything, including electronics but also checks. I could cash them. People get drivers licenses, birth certificates, debit cards, just about anything that could be sent from here to there.

I thought of access—*when* to do it. A million things at once raced through my mind. Had I just unlocked a treasure chest? Or would I drown opening it? Time would tell. I called it "the golden key."

And I thought of the consequences, though not for very long. This would be a federal offense, and I would become the target of the FBI, which was precisely what happened. When I started to use that key, I had to run harder, faster, and smarter. Eventually, that exact key was what got me caught and put in the federal pen for many years. I will write more about my captivity in another chapter.

I decided it was easier to follow that van driver on his route than to figure out which drop-off boxes this key opened and where they were located. I knew about what time he emptied the box on the corner by the Exxon station. I went back there and waited the next day. Sure enough, about the same time, he parked his large van at that spot, emptied the blue box, and went on his way. I was on his tail.

Not too many people follow delivery personnel, but I did stay a block or so away, so not to raise suspicion. After he picked up the parcels at Exxon Mobil, he went to several additional businesses near there.

He would park his vehicle and, with a bunch of packages in his hands, walk into a business and deliver them, sometimes pick up parcels, and get back to his vehicle. No use of the key there.

After hitting about a dozen businesses, he took a right into a residential neighborhood. There, he delivered to residential houses, walking to the front doors. No use for a key there.

He continued in that neighborhood hitting many residences. Sometimes, he would get out and leave a parcel on the front door. He used some kind of handheld computer to scan a barcode. I could hear the confirmation beep when I got close.

When he was finished with this neighborhood, he came out the same street he came in and went across the street. There was a large apartment complex with three sections of wall-mounted drop-off boxes.

Bingo. When he got out of the vehicle, he used the same key that was attached to his belt to swing open a large drop-off box and picked up small and large parcels and boxes of checks—just as I was hoping for. I could hardly contain my glee.

Then he swung the large door shut and opened the next one. He did this with three different boxes in that area. Wow, I was amazed, shocked, and exhilarated. The possibilities of financially viable items could open up a whole new world of riches and false identities to me.

Later, I learned that a delivery person in Los Angeles was killed by a man who was only interested in that golden key. The street value for that key was about $5,000. But if somebody offered me the same amount of money for it, I wouldn't have taken it. I had much bigger plans.

I followed that person for almost the entire remaining part of the day. He also had many more of those drop-off boxes that he emptied that day, most of them at the end of his route.

Then he came to a newly developed subdivision with very expensive homes. Believe it or not, those rich people did not have boxes in front of their house like the older middle-class neighborhoods. There, he picked up more boxes than usual. I guess those people had computers, prepared their own labels, and dropped their parcels in the drop-off box to be shipped across the country. Some people must have run a business from their home, mailing many packages of the same size wrapped in the same brown paper.

This golden key provided a lucrative source of income for me for about a year.

I would pick a day of the week, around the first of the month. I would find more checks and go to the drop-off boxes, usually early in the morning, around 4:00 a.m., knowing that most people were still asleep in their beds, and I would empty as many as I could find. I'd start with the one on the corner of the Exxon station, the one that had "shown me the light," so to speak.

Then on other days, about the same time, at 4:00 a.m., when most sensible people were sawing logs, I would go to the apartment complexes and swing open the large drop-off boxes and take what I could carry.

I would find credit card renewals and the pin numbers in the same drop-off boxes the next day. I stole whole boxes of checkbooks. With my false identity kits, consisting of wigs, glasses, mustaches, and the like, I could easily write those checks and buy what I wanted. I mailed them to people and had the items I purchased mailed to a PO box that I opened with stolen money and only kept for a week.

To live legally, you have to have a driver's license and vehicle insurance. It was ironic, but I used a stolen driver's license, taken from a drop-off box, to open a business, and paid for the business permit with a stolen check. And I got away with it all, at least I thought so—until the Federal Inspection Service began digging in my past. I did pay for that with some federal time.

Listen to this, Houston.

These delivery services do deliver! They are conscientious about screening and hiring people who honestly deliver the items you ordered and wanted. The money Aunt Helen sent to you, she really did send it. But I stole it before it got to you.

I *un*delivered it. All over Houston, when they delivered it, I stole it. And by the time you figured it out, it was long gone, and so was I. And when you started calling them, asking, "Where is my parcel?" and complaining that the company hadn't done its job and delivered your package, you were wrong. The company *did* deliver it, and the driver scanned it delivered. The reason it's *not* in your possession is that I stole it before you got there.

My apologies, all you hardworking delivery personnel.

My apologies for the confusion, Houston.

As I told you earlier, those drop-off boxes in the upscale neighborhoods were a particularly rich source of income. A lot of valuable items are delivered by and to them.

Plus, they're too lazy to get off their genuine leather sectionals while they watch their oval LCD TVs. They order from catalogs or online and get it shipped to them. Well, they try. But in these neighborhoods, my golden key provided me with lots of Christmas presents all year long.

The delivery person would sort the parcels by neighborhood, put them in the back of his van, and deliver the goods to your neighborhood box. Since the parcel was too big, he would scan the parcel *delivered* and leave it in a drop-off box. But I beat you to it. I stole at least a dozen parcels each night when I used this flawless scheme.

I can just imagine your frustration when your smart phone notified you of the delivery date and time. You couldn't wait to get off work to swing by on the way home and pick up your parcel and that gadget you so desperately wanted (but did not really need). You retrieved the key, opened the drop-off box, and *nothing was there.* Steaming hot, you attempted to call the delivery service. Sorry, they closed at 5:00 p.m.

You called the national complaint line, who started a case, which would show up on the supervisor computer the next morning. He'd print it out; it would say something like, "I ordered this item. The tracking shows it traveling to Houston, arriving at our local branch, and delivered at 10:00 a.m. yesterday morning, but it was not there."

The supervisor would approach the person who had that route that day and make an inquiry of his or her actions. The employee would swear up and down that he or she delivered the parcel to the right box and scanned it at so-and-so time.

The supervisor would then call you and either give you some lame excuse or just tell you what the employee said and try to calm you down. They did not have the answer *or* the parcel.

By this time, it was safely at my house, stacked up with all kinds of items I really didn't need but could pawn fairly easily. I had accumulated so many cardboard boxes in the process I could have started my own parcel store. I eventually had to flatten them out and deposit them in the local recycle bin. You have to save the world, you know, recycle.

This went on for a long time.

That was my mistake; there started to be an accumulation of lost parcel cases. The inspectors were becoming very suspicious. They'd plotted the missing items on a map and concluded that not all the delivery employees were stealing parcels, checks, credit/debit cards, and cash. Rather, the missing items were concentrated in a particular zone, the one I had the key for. Among those deliver workers, 99 percent of were hardworking men and women who just wanted to do a job, go home, and pay the bills to raise their families.

The inspectors really didn't care that much that I was stealing all this stuff, but they realized I had that golden key, and they wanted that key back. Otherwise, they would have to change a bunch of locks. I never realized when I broke into that safe that the most valuable item I'd get was a small item hanging on the wall. In another chapter, I will tell you more about making fake IDs and how I used the items of nonmonetary value to continue my illegal quest.

First, let me tell you how I got caught.

I had two sisters, one of whom died suddenly; she was married to an alcoholic, so I ended up taking this seventeen-year-old kid in. His name was Frederic, but everybody called him Fred. The family thought it was a good idea at the time. I had a successful job, they thought. I lived in a beautiful part of town, near the Galleria, on the top floor in a penthouse. It covered the whole eighteenth floor; the view was amazing from up there. But I mentored Fred in the fine art of thievery. Of the seven deadly sins, I stayed away from six but specialized in one, *greed*—in getting what I wanted without paying. And Fred was an eager student.

We had just emptied a drop-off box in a neighborhood and had four garbage bags full of parcels on the backseat of our car. I was driving a light blue Delta 88, with a dark blue vinyl roof; it was two-door. I always liked those six-foot long doors. It had a back seat, and you had to fold the front seats forward to get in there. The rear windows were very small and tinted as dark as possible. I was hoping that, since the back seat was somewhat obscured, nobody would be able to see our loot in the back.

I'm not sure why the cop pulled us over. With these hot cars that I bought from questionable sources, anything could be wrong. It might have had a missing taillight; there isn't a lot of quality control at that "dealership."

When he pulled us over, we had garbage bags full of parcels on the back seat. I told my nephew to deny everything. We had a lot of items that were illegally obtained from drop-off boxes.

Yes, officer. No, officer. Yes, officer. Fred did not say a word. I had a false driver's license on me, with a different name, but my picture was indistinguishable from a real one. I had the equipment and was good at using it. I will tell you more about that later when I describe my apartment.

When he searched the car and found all those parcels, he became very suspicious. He arrested both of us, put us in handcuffs, and took us to the police station.

While I was sitting in my handcuffs in the back of the police cruiser, I took the credit cards I'd just stolen and that golden key that I'd stolen from that safe (the same key that had given me access to parcels for a year). I shoved both in the back seat of the car behind me, between the seat and the back; they slid right in there.

When we arrived at the police station, the arresting officer put us in a room, made us empty our pockets, and poured the contents of the garbage bags on long white tables. There were piles of boxes of all sizes. He asked us where we'd gotten all of them. I lied and told him the car didn't belong to me; it was a friend's car, and we had no idea how the bag had gotten there.

This was definitely out of his jurisdiction, so he called the Inspection Service. Within an hour, Mr. Jones arrived and introduced himself as an inspector of the Houston area. He asked us where we'd gotten the parcels; I told him the same lie.

He asked me, "What would I find if I obtained a search warrant for your house?"

I answered him, "Nothing!"

My thoughts raced again. I almost freaked out, I had been on a yearlong streak of stealing parcels, massive amounts, and Houston was a big city. My house was loaded with stolen items and many boxes, some not even opened yet. Some were just plain brown boxes. Others were white, red, and blue boxes. Those boxes are free when you mail stuff, and they all look the same. They usually have more valuable contents than the plain brown ones. And now and then, I had found overnight parcels. They missed a lot of overnight deliveries in the Houston area because of me. Apologies, Houston. You did do your job, but I undid it.

Those overnight parcels were usually worth it. They contained contracts sometimes or legal documents. But often they contained checks or money orders or large amounts of cash and sometimes car keys.

One very special item I found several times in the overnight envelopes were keys. You know when you go to Grandma's house with your wife and kids. Then when you leave, you forget your car keys at Grandma's, but you have your wife's keys and use them to drive home. Then Grandma calls and says, 'I found your keys, son!' Well, she is in Dallas, and the three-hour drive (one way) isn't worth it. You ask Grandma to overnight them to you; it is guaranteed overnight. And she does.

But since I had the ability to open neighborhood drop-off boxes and empty them between the time they were delivered and the time you got home, your vehicle key will not be there as was guaranteed. There will be no key for you, as I have it, even though the tracking said it was delivered.

I often wondered how many angry customers called the Houston parcel delivery businesses and how their deliveries and delivery failures showed up in the performance indicators. Did it show a substantial decrease in successful deliveries in Houston because I stayed swamped, grabbing your parcels before you did?

This provided a large amount of income. The car lot where I bought all my (stolen) cars was always in need of new wheels. And since I had the keys and the exact address this vehicle was located (because your name and address were on the overnight envelope and your car key was in it), I could go there any time I wanted to and drive it off. A garage door usually presented not so much of a hindrance; I owned a multichannel garage door opener. It could scan 175 frequencies and codes in thirty seconds and would open the garage door as I drove up.

Unless there was a dog in the garage, I opened the driver's door with the key, started the vehicle, and sped off—no alarms, no broken windows. In one year, I stole eighteen vehicles with keys obtained from the stolen parcels—two BMWs, four Chevy Tahoes, one Volkswagen Jetta, four pickup trucks, three Jeeps, and four others. Selling those cars to the traveling car lot greatly contributed to my enterprising life.

This golden key I lifted out of that safe made me about $100,000 in one year. But eventually, I lost it. Well, I hid it in the police cruiser. I sure would miss that key.

The policeman totally left us under the care and responsibility of the inspector. He was stern and asked us a lot of questions. Fred hardly said anything, just like I'd told him. I gave evasive answers. I definitely had the gift of gab and could talk myself out of a lot of situations, which is better than shooting your way out, I guess.

I don't remember much of his end of the conversation. But I remember one thing—what he told me at the end just before he let both of us go.

He said, "If you're lying, I will catch you. It might take me a while, but I will catch you!"

And eventually, he did. That key actually got me caught.

Much later, when they detailed the police cruiser—it was cleaned by guys in the county jail, in fact—the cleaners found the credit cards and that golden key. It had my fingerprints on it.

At that time, I was locked up in this unit in Livingston for another offense. Go figure.

The feds came in. I was called to the warden's office. The warden said, "The feds are here, and they are going to take you away. There is nothing I can do about it. They have a federal case on you."

Mr. Jones was there, smiling. He didn't say, "I told you so!" But his facial expression said everything. They had their key back; my crime spree was halted. Perhaps now, Houston, you can get your credit cards and packages delivered like normal.

The evidence was overwhelming. I got a ten-year federal sentence added to my time. The authorities were not happy with what I had done. Crime does not pay, at least not for very long.

CHAPTER 7

BOOBY-TRAPPED PAWNSHOPS

If you have any hints or feelings about starting a career in crime, particularly stealing, my advice is to stay away from pawnshops. Yes, they do have a lot of stuff, but they are somewhat determined to keep it. I heard of one guy robbing a pawnshop during the day, who raised his gun and made a threat. He was shot from five different directions—yes, dead.

That is why I only approached pawnshops at nighttime. The gun-toting owners would be gone, but they often left surprises behind—booby traps and obstacles. One such trap almost got me killed one time. But then I learned. And since I do like a challenge and pawnshops did have a lot of valuable merchandise (that I could easy pawn somewhere else), I continued to rob them, usually successfully.

Pawnshop number one

One Pawnshop I visited was on the corner of Westheimer Road and Fountain View Drive. First, I would go there and pawn something. A week later, I would make half the payment to get it back. Then the next week, I would get it back out of pawn. Often, I would pawn an electronic item I'd stolen from the parcels, like a smart phone or tablet, or a Rolex watch from the judge's house.

Every time I went there, I observed the layout, the counters, how many employees, where the computers and cash were, and if I could see the safes. I would make a mental note of everything, write it down when I could, go home, and draw a floor plan as detailed as possible. This way, I would have the perfect layout of the building. Not only would I draw it, but during that process, I would also get familiar with entrances and exits. This gave me the confidence to break in, do my business, and get out.

Pawnshops were usually not in the best part of town and were often kept protected with motion detectors and/or other ways and means to either keep you out or disable you when you are there.

This one pawnshop had a single glass front door and square windows along the wall. It was an adobe-style, white plastered wall with blue trim around the windows. I liked that the windows were small—not too much visibility from the street.

I came back at night; went to the back of the building; and clipped the phone lines from the box in the back, disabling the alarm. I parked my truck as close to the door as I could. It was a solid steel door that opened to the inside. I knew I could not tackle the door. But above the door was a three-foot-wide, two-foot high window. It was the only window in the back, and it gave the shop a little natural light to work in. It gave me a little glass to work with, for which I was grateful.

Standing on the roof of the truck, I used my glass cutters and suction cup and cut a perfect two-foot circle in the glass. With a few hits of a very small ball peen hammer attached to my belt, the loosening crack raced around the circle, and the suction cup allowed me to pull it safely toward me. I lay it in the back of my truck and climbed in the window.

Through practice and experience, I learned that, if I went headfirst, I could hold on to the edge of the window with my feet and often touch the iron of the roof beams and swing from them, lowering myself right behind the back door. Sometimes, hanging from my feet, I could open the door from the inside with ease.

Not tonight, I slipped through the hole, lost my grip, and fell on the cement, landing on my hands and feet. My head almost hit the ground. I barely caught myself and ended up almost flat on the floor—which was a good thing.

While I fell, a shotgun went off.

Bang.

It made my ears ring.

It left a pattern of pellets on the back of the steel gray door, indenting the door in hundreds of places—right in the place where I would have stood if I'd have opened the door with my hands.

The pawnshop owners had installed an illegal burglary prevention device. The trigger of the shotgun was connected to the back door with a rope. Anybody who opened that back door would, by that motion, pull the trigger and shoot themselves to smithereens. I had never seen it exactly like that before. I lay trembling on the floor—thinking how lucky I was that I had fallen.

This meant revenge. I only wanted to steal the pawnshop contents, but they seemed intent on wanting to kill me. I went to work quickly, first making sure there were no other guns hooked up to tripwires.

The front of the store had many large windows. I couldn't venture in the front at all. But the safe was in the storeroom. You know, that's the area where they put stuff that was pawned, but they can't sell it yet.

I opened the back door and grabbed the Stihl grinding wheel out of my truck. After studying the safe for a minute, I marked the target opening and cranked up the machine.

The door of that old safe was no match for my faithful companion. Within an hour, I had full access to all the gold and diamond watches and rings I wanted. I loaded up my backpack, stuffed it full, and carefully zipped it shut. I wiped off any surfaces

I had possibly touched, even though I always wore black leather gloves, and loaded my truck. I kept the grinding wheel in the back seat and my backpack on the left front floorboard.

I went back one more time. I opened all the faucets, stopped up the toilet with a bunch of leather gloves, opened the cover on the back of the toilets, disabled the floats, and flushed it. This allowed four faucets to run as fast as possible, hopefully flooding the place by the time 8:00 a.m. came around.

Normally, I did not do this. It was not my signature, but that shotgun booby trap got my goat. I decided to fight fire with water. First, I thought about torching the place, but there were too many residences nearby. I didn't want to be picked up for arson or attempted murder. This pawnshop owner should have been arrested for attempted murder, for mounting this gun right in my line of travel. I closed the door behind me and drove off.

Pawnshop number two

Another one of my nightly ventures in the pawnshop robbery business ended up in a mess.

This pawnshop, at Bellfort Road and Cullen Street, had double glass doors. When I visited there a few times, I could tell there were no holes in the top of the door frame or in the bottom in the cement. That meant the door only had a lock in the middle. But it was a strong modern lock and not one I could easily pick.

Again, the first things I did on arriving at the pawnshop, the easy way to prevent visitors, was go to the back of the building and disable all the phone lines running into the building. Why people don't secure those, I don't know. I should go to work as a security specialist.

Then I did something I had never done, hoping this would provide me quick access. The only reason I thought about doing this was because the main entrance of this pawnshop was not facing the road but, rather, on the side of the building. I drove my truck carefully with the front bumper against the middle of the two doors and inched forward. What I expected to happen happened. The doors both popped open with a loud bang. I was afraid the glass would bust, but it didn't. I turned my truck sideways and parked as if I was an employee on the night shift.

I took my Stihl grinder and my backpack out and entered the building. I found a chain in a for-sale bin, tied the door shut from the inside, and walked to the back. I knew where the safe was and went to work. But somehow, they had modified the door—unbeknownst to me.

I made four marks on the door and started cutting, first the top. The red glow of the diamond wheel made a smooth two-foot cut near the top of the safe. Then I started on the right side, as usual.

I was about halfway down when I hit something I was not supposed to hit. It grabbed my blade and saw; broke the blade, shattering it; and threw the saw out of my hands. It landed on the floor with the motor still running.

The blade had come apart, and one of the sections had shot right at me. The speed and rotation of the disk threw the razor-sharp part of the blade toward me. It went from the saw, under my wrists, protected by my glove, but then made a serious gash in my underarm and stuck there.

My arm was cut badly. I usually did not panic. But worriedly, I had to abandon my thievery. I removed the piece of blade from my arm, grabbed a rag lying nearby, and wrapped it around my arm to prevent it from getting worse. I picked up the saw, undid the chain from the front, and got out of there as soon as I could.

It is a good thing I knew a doctor who had an examination room in his house. He had a successful practice and was on the board of MD Anderson. I'm not sure why he did this—because he was single or because he had a strange infatuation with the underworld maybe. But whatever the reason, he was well known by the people I associated with. Any time day or night he would treat you.

He would even leave his practice, leaving all his honest patients in the waiting room. The nurses would tell you he'd been called to emergency surgery and had to reschedule everybody there. It was emergency surgery sure enough, but often if it was sewing up bullet wounds received during a robbery. He asked you a lot of questions about your life, your outlook on life, your vision for the future, and if you had peace doing this. But he never asked you how you got hurt. He just helped you; he was a very kind man indeed. And he took watches as payment.

I went to his house and rang the doorbell. He was home. He opened the door slowly. When he saw the wrap around my arm, he knew I needed immediate care. He whisked me into the hidden part of the house, where, behind large bookshelves, was a door that rotated and revealed what looked like a doctor's office and an operating room.

He told me to lie down and carefully unwrapped the wound. As soon as it was uncovered it, he shook his head. He put pressure on the vein, stopping the wound instantly. Then he pulled out a syringe with a very thin needle and gave me several shots—tetanus, I believe, and painkiller. I had my eyes open, but that needle was so thin I didn't even feel it go through my skin.

The pain started to go away almost instantly; he proceeded to clean the wound. When he needed both hands to treat me, he told me where to put pressure.

When he was cleaning the wound, he found bits of the shattered diamond blade in the wound. Was I happy to have expert care and not an amateur.

He poured peroxide on it first and then iodine. He let it soak in for a while. Then he started stitching it with a round needle and a long black string, holding it tightly closed. I was in his office for about an hour and a half.

I paid him with one of the most expensive watches I'd stolen from the judge's house. We were both pleased with the exchange.

He was a watch aficionado. I knew he really liked the ones with the rotating cages—tourbillion, he called them.

He walked me to the door, giving me a bottle of antibiotics and told me to come back in a week, but not at this midnight hour. I shook his left hand, as my right arm was in a sling.

The next morning, I went back to the same pawnshop, milled around for a while, and bought an iPod classic. It is amazing how much people run their mouths. From the clerks, I found out everything I wanted to know.

They told me how they'd come to work and found the proof of an attempted burglary. Somebody had attempted to crack their safe. They explained how the inside of the door of the safe was rigged so that, if somebody tried to do what the burglar did, it would send a hardened object quickly toward the inside of the door with an electric actuator.

That was how I'd found out why something *hit* the grinder and kicked it back at me, breaking the blade in the process. That little booby trap could have killed me also. By the way, I took my arm out of the sling before I went to the pawnshop.

I did not want to be like the arsonist who goes to revel in the blazing fire he just set. They might have been on the lookout for somebody with a large wound. At least the local emergency wouldn't turn me into the police department, and there was no 9-1-1 record of my call.

Pawnshop number 3

Why pawnshops have such a propensity to set booby traps, I don't know. Perhaps it's that they deal with that part of society like me—those who steal items and try to get money for them. Perhaps it's because they deal with people who don't respect the law, so they don't either.

The third pawnshop, on N McCarthy Street, just outside 610 Loop, did a similar thing. By this time, I had been forewarned. This was, perhaps, pawnshop SOP. I didn't know.

The third pawnshop I robbed had a large steel door in the back. The front seemed impenetrable, with iron bars behind the glass. It is hard to remove those iron bars unless you remove the whole glass plate. The back door seemed to be a more reasonable access point for me.

I'd created a large grapple hook. It was a one-inch steel pipe about four feet long. I welded a bulldog trailer hitch to one end. On the other end, I cut two holes for bolts, one near the top and one a little further down, at a ninety-degree angle. Then I cut slits in the pipe about two feet long and attached flat pieces of iron to the bolts, two pieces of iron on each side of one bolt and two pieces of iron on each side of the other bolt. The iron folded into the pipe, filling the slots perfectly.

A little after midnight, I approached the back door of this pawnshop on Westheimer. There was a bright orange halogen security light that lit up the back of the pawnshop. I used a pellet gun and popped it; the pellet gun was silent and busted the bulb in a thousand pieces. It snowed glass and white powder for a minute; I could see the white dust from the inside coating of the light falling in the moonlight.

Having secured my invisibility, I backed my truck to about five feet from the door. With a large battery-powered drill, I made a one and a quarter-inch hole in the back door. The door had a very sturdy frame, but the body was of inferior, thin material. The drill did its work very quietly; I sprayed W40 on the drill bit now and then to keep it from squealing. The drill bit quickly penetrated the thin outer layer; the core of the door was made of particle board, which was dispatched with quickly. The inner steel layer was a little bit thicker than the outer one. But within ten minutes, I had penetrated the door completely.

I laid the drill and oil back in the bed of the truck and picked up my homemade grapple hook and attached it to the back of the truck. One of the pins folded down and kept it at the right level. I got in my truck and backed the iron pipe through the hole and then pulled a rope through the middle of the pipe. This extended the four pieces of iron out like the propellers of a helicopter.

First, I looked around and listened to ensure nobody was watching or listening. I didn't hear any sirens, footsteps, or voices. Then with my truck in four-wheel drive, I inched it forward. The grapple hook slowly pulled the door off its hinges, and it popped out of, its frame landing on the back of my truck. Voilà, a homemade key. I detached the door from the grapple hook, which was quite a job. The door was heavy; I might want to use the hook again sometime.

I stepped into the pawnshop. This one did not have a large footprint. There were a lot of shelves all around the walls. On one side, they were filled mostly with tools. The other side was all electronics. Toward the front glass were large toolboxes and tires. What I was more interested in was that the whole inside was a double ring of jewelry displays. For a thief like me, gold and diamonds are an easy commodity. Such items were easy to take apart, transform, melt, and do whatever it took to transform them into something that was not recognizable to the previous owner.

During the night, of course, the shelves were empty, and everything was in the safe. I'd glanced at the safe from the side and recognized the brand and type. Like I said before, when I was in prison and studied locksmithing, I also received a book on safes and construction. This safe was easy to get into; I didn't have to burn open the door. Rather, I could use drill bits in certain critical places, according to my instruction book.

Before I stepped into the building, I sprayed a can of smoke inside the building, put on a pair of sunglasses with modified lenses, and could see red lines across the floor. There were laser tripwires throughout the building. I stepped over them carefully. The phone lines were disabled, but I didn't know if breaking the laser beam would pull another trigger to a shotgun or an Uzi or worse.

There were two safes in the building, a four-foot square old green safe on large iron casters and a walk-in safe. I recognized the make and model of the old square safe. This was an old safe that could be opened by drilling the metal cage that holds the lock at an exact location. I measured from the center of the dial. It had to be precise, for which I used a caliper. I marked one white X where I needed to punch my hole. To keep you from being tempted to become a safecracker, let me keep the other locations off limits for you right now.

For this job, I brought a DeWalt18 volt battery-operated drill with three battery packs and titanium drill bits. I marked the location and drilled two pilot holes, with a regular drill bit. This was where I attached my drill "stand" to the door of the safe—similar to a drill press used in machine shops. Usually, they're vertical, about six feet tall, with a strong motor and a work table below the bit where you can securely fasten the item you're drilling in.

This rig was similar and smaller, but horizontal. It allowed me to "SET" the drill in the stand and slowly progress forward, drilling in the same angle and position and using a wheel with three handles to crawl the drill and bit towards the door and also allow me to put just the right amount of pressure on the drill bit while sitting comfortably on a five-gallon bucket.

I inserted my first drill bit and made pretty good headway through the door. I could tell this was a quality old safe, with carbon-reinforced steel. I wore out the first bit in five minutes. I usually carried ten of them. These are locksmith drill bits. They're about the size of a pencil. The bit isn't pointed but, rather, round like a straw and covered with diamond dust.

You remember going to the ear, nose, and throat specialist? They have a device that allows them to look into your ear and nose. They hold the handle on the side and peep through the lens in the back. A light shines down into the hole, allowing them to see what's going on down there. I used the same device to look down the hole I was drilling to check on progress and to study the layers of material this safe was made of.

I changed drill bits. The new bit made a difference immediately. I could tell I'd made good progress. I also blew away the shaving with a can of compressed air.

After three more bits, I hit pay dirt. Or actually, I hit nothing, which let me know I was now below and to the front of the tumblers. With the ear scope, I could see the brass plates that make up the heart of the lock. These plates have a trapezoid cut out of them in a specific location. Those have to align perfectly to open the safe. When they're aligned, it allows for a rod to fall in the gutter the aligned cutouts make, and then the rod falls away. You can turn the large handle that pulls the pins out of both sides of the door. That's all it took—a drill, a few bits, and a scope—and voilà, I was inside.

I cracked the door open a little bit and saw something not totally unexpected but not something I usually saw or wanted to see. The owners of the pawnshop had tied a tripwire to the inside of the door. On the other end of the wire in the middle of the safe, there was a hand grenade. I am telling you, these pawnshop owners were desperate. Didn't they know owning a hand grenade was illegal? If I had opened the door, I would have been hit with hot green cast-iron shrapnel. I clipped the wire to the hand grenade, saving it for later. The door swung open. There were half a dozen metal trays and four square compartments, two on the bottom and two below.

With a crowbar, I popped all the drawers open and emptied the contents into my duffel bag. There were loads of rings, some with diamonds, some without and many necklaces. I kept shoving things into my bag. There were watches of all kinds, some of them too old and too out of date to worry about, some with lots of bling.

The bottom compartments had two dozen pistols, wrapped in black cloth. After I added the pistols to my duffel bag, the bag became almost too heavy to pick up.

I was anxious to open the walk-in safe. I know you are going to have a hard time believing how I opened this one.

On my last visit as an honest customer to that pawnshop, I observed that, if you stood at the electronic department of the store, you had a clear view of their main walk-in safe from the right. I took a deer camera from one of their shelves and set it between two TVs. It was hardly visible, I turned it on, making sure it had working batteries and an SD card and that it recorded an mp4 file when any motion was detected.

The next day I came back and bought the deer camera, took it home, and viewed the mp4 file on my laptop. It was almost beyond belief. It showed the manager at the end of the day taking all the cash drawers from his clerks who worked the counters. I could clearly observe him rotating the dials on the safe, right three times, stopping at a number; left two times, stopping at another number; right one time, stopping at another number; and then left, stopping at zero.

This was almost too easy. It was unbelievable; with his own tools, he'd given me the combination of the safe. I didn't have to see the number on the top. From the side view, I could extrapolate what the top number would be and wrote them down. Here I went—21, 53, 64, 0. I could tell by the resistance going towards the zero that this safe was "cracked." And sure enough, I could turn the large handle on the left of the dial from horizontal to vertical, disengaging the one-inch chrome bars and withdrawing them into the door. The door swung open. No drill, no dynamite; just an SD card provided me access to the door.

Here was his operating capital, almost $250,000 in stacks of bills. There were many neat piles of one hundred-dollar bills, some fifties and many twenties and tens. I filled my second duffel bag. It looked like something from a bank robbery movie, but this was genuine money. There was still plenty of room for the little black velvet bags with loose diamonds and the red and black coral necklaces, cultured pearl earrings, and too many rings to count.

Another surprising find was old coins. This pawnshop owner, fearing a financial breakdown, most have been a long time numismatic. In individual plastic covers a little smaller than a credit card were hundreds of coins. The description was written on indentation in the card each coin was being held in, including the approximate year of origin. There were price stickers on the back. Some of these coins were from the days of the Roman Empire with the image of Caesar stamped on the coin.

I knew a "hot" coin collector who would give me a fair street price for these coins, so I stuffed my duffel back full. The zipper barely closed, and it also became hard to carry.

It was time to leave, a good catch for one night. I estimated my sweep netted me around $500,000. Not bad for a day's work. Most blue-collar workers would have to work eight years to make that. It took me a little bit of preparation and two hours of hard work. Now you understand how I could afford a fancy high-rise. I made quick money and invested it wisely.

CHAPTER 8

I WAS SHOT!

When you rob businesses, it is better to rob one with a lot of money. But the owners usually don't have a sign hanging out the window that says, "Lots of money in the safe tonight."

I'm sure you heard of the Texas Seven. They robbed an Oshman's Sporting Goods store during the busy Christmas season, hoping to land a big catch. Their plans were a little fouled up when a security guard noticed something unusual at that store. He paid with his life, and all of the seven, except one, ended up on Death Row in Livingston, Texas. (The seventh committed suicide.)

As a thief, you are presented with the same problem all the time. You don't exactly know who has money *when*. I just had to take my chances.

I made plans to rob a car parts store one night. I'd scouted the location out before, and it looked like the store was doing good business. While there, I also observed its alarm system; it was one I was familiar with, easy to disable.

Because I expected a fairly large haul, I asked an associate of mine to help us rob this place. He spoke with a strong Texas accent, and I always called him Bubba. He never objected.

The parts store was located at 8199Short Point Road in Houston. It was visible from the road, but there were a lot of bushes on the side that would prohibit a passing police car from staring into the store.

Our plan of attack was to be in the back of the parking lot right at dark. We were in a black Lincoln Continental, Bubba was driving, my wife and I were in the back seat. This sleigh had a huge trunk; we expected large loot.

The parking lot was dark due to insufficient lighting. The first thing I did was find the phone line and clip it, disabling the communication of the alarm to central control and the police. Then we drove away and waited five minutes. If the communications had a reverse tracking back to the store, it would sound an alarm anyway. If within five minutes there was no police activity, we had a clear zone till dawn.

A quick trip to Starbucks inside the Kroger twenty-four-hour store on Wirt Road gave us five minutes and some caffeine to keep us awake during the night, even if the adrenaline wouldn't be enough.

We went to work. I cracked open the back door with a slightly modified floor jack. It had sharp points and a hydraulic plunger that slowly separated the door from the doorjamb. The alarm control was close to the back door. When the back door popped open, I'd have about fifteen seconds to disable it. I did it in ten. The store was ours now.

My wife stayed outside to watch for suspicious activity. We had radios on us to keep in contact.

Bubba went through the store, looking for valuable tools and parts. I went to the office and targeted the safe.

After a while, my wife came on the radio. "What is he doing?" she said.

I said, "What do you mean?"

She said, "He's carrying stuff from the store to the middle of the parking lot!'

I left the safe and went to the store shelves. Sure enough, Bubba was carrying arms full of tools, light bulbs, quarts of oil—just anything he could grab and carry—and was making a pile behind the store in the middle of the parking lot. I asked him if he was losing it; he said he needed the stuff.

It usually does not pay to argue with stubborn people, so I let him do his thing. I asked him to make a separate pile of toolboxes, the plastic ones that are filled with two sets of open-end wrenches, one side metric, the other side SAE and some with socket wrenches in both sizes. These were items that were easily carried—they had handles—and they would be easily sold in any pawnshop. Guys are always looking for a deal on tools.

The pile got higher and higher, but I didn't care. I went back to the safe.

This was a safe I didn't recognize. It was newer, with material and construction different than any I'd ever seen. My regular drill bit would not work, as I had no idea where the locking mechanism was in the safe door and how to access it. I would need to read up on this one. I couldn't let this happen again; they'd snuck one up on me. I wrote the model number in my notebook.

I retrieved my Stihl cutting wheel from the car and cranked it up. The safe was fairly centrally located in the back of the store. I had the muffler stuffed with some steel wool and fiberglass insulation. It was fairly quiet. It did not make much more noise than a warm hand dryer like they have in the bathroom at McDonalds.

I made four cuts in the door in a rectangle, the top and bottom cuts about twelve inches wide, the sides about twenty inches. All I needed was a hole large enough to stick my hands through. Sparks flew everywhere, and the building was filling with exhaust. As a precaution, I disabled the carbon dioxide and smoke detectors. I didn't want the fire department to surprise us with a cold shower.

After about an hour of cutting, I was in. First, I had to let the door cool off. The heat from the cutting had traveled all the way to the edges; iron is a good heat conductor. Eventually, the hole was cool enough for me to reach inside the door and inside the safe. With my scope, I studied the locking mechanism mounted in the top right corner of the safe. I could barely reach the locking pin that controlled the rest of the bars and reset it. Now the handle turned, and the bars that I hadn't cut through actually retracted into the door. One I had to pull out with a large vise grip. One I had to use a hammer and a little more gentle persuasion to retract out of the wall back into the door. But then Ali Baba and his forty thieves procured their treasure.

I was very disappointed. There was only about $5,000 in bills in that safe. There were several proprietary company manuals and CDs and spare keys to the rest of the building and—coins, a lot of them.

Perhaps parts customers paid with large bills for small parts, and they need a lot of change in this store. The pennies and nickels were modest in value and effort. But the dimes and quarters would be a nice asset to contribute to the payday that night.

There was a canvas bag with loose dimes about the size of a gallon of milk and two bags of quarters about the same size. One bag was totally full and one was half full. I switched some of the contents of the full bag of quarters to the other one. Now they both were about three-quarters full. I took the ends of the canvas bags, looped them through my belt and put a knot in the top, one on my left hip and one on my right. I felt like a pack mule. On each hip I had about $1,000 worth of each bag weighing close to fifty pounds

The bag of dimes I gave to my wife, waiting outside. She put it in her purse and wrapped it around my shoulder.

While I was cracking the safe, Bubba had created an unmanageable mountain of parts in the parking lot. But he'd stacked the tool boxes neatly beside the disaster mountain. I laid my tools by the back door and got the car, first loading my tools on the back seat in the middle. Then we loaded the trunk and the back seat full of tool boxes and told him to drive.

He said, "What about the other stuff?"

I told him, "Forget about it!"

He said, "OK"

He got into the driver's seat, and my wife got in next, sitting in the middle. I sat near the passenger door. These Continentals had a nice bench seat all the way across, with plenty of seat for three average size persons. With a large 8 cylinder engine, we had plenty of power to haul this heavy load. The rear end was a little lower. It was night and the low beams would blind oncoming traffic.

We took a left on Westheimer, stayed on Westheimer for three blocks, and took a left on Post Oak Boulevard. It was 4:00 a.m., not a whole lot of residential traffic. We had a red light on Post Oak Boulevard. The rear of the car was really loaded down with toolboxes, the headlights were pointing up a little too much. On the opposite side, waiting at the light, was a police car. Our headlights were shining through his front window, illuminating his face.

I'm not sure why Bubba panicked, maybe because he lit up the cop. Perhaps it was because he didn't get his way about hauling the big pile of lamps and other parts he'd created. Perhaps it was the lights blinding the officers and lighting up their car like a Christmas tree in July. Whatever the case, he panicked and floored the Continental, flying through a red light jumped up, and had us going sixty miles per hour on Post Oak before you could say, "Chase us!"

The cop was paying attention. Why not? There was nobody else at the light. And eating doughnuts all night long probably gets boring also. He whipped around and was on our tail in no time. Most of these cop cars have turbos added to their motors, turning them into racing machines.

Here we were, running again—running in the dark, with an insane man piloting our getaway car.

You'd never guess what he did. He kept stopping at stop signs. The police car behind us had its lights flashing and siren going, making us increasingly more aware of his presence and a lot more nervous. We also knew he had already called for backup, and more of these fast black-and-whites were headed our direction from all corners of the earth. We had a better chance evading one team than multiple men in blue.

I told my wife we are going to make a run for it. She said, "OK." The next time Bubba stopped at a stop sign, we bolted, running out of the car and into a residential neighborhood. He had taken a right on San Felipe, raced under the West 610 loop, and almost lost control turning left on Post Oak Park Drive.

When he slowed down a little, I jumped out, dragging my wife out with me. The certainty of her getting caught with Bubba was more of a risk than the few scratches and bumps we would get jumping out of a running car. We got up and started running away from the road in the dark.

Unbeknownst to us, we were in Audubon Park Community, one of the more exclusive gated communities in Houston, located inside the loop. Most of the Gold Coast had moved further away from the crime center. These rich people had constructed their own castle inside the criminal war zone, and we ran into it.

We ran through an open gate into a private driveway with a four-car garage to our right and shrubs right in front of us with a cedar fence between that house and the neighbor.

One of the policemen had left the vehicle and given chase on foot. He couldn't see us very well, but he could hear us running. He fired at us.

It's not fun getting shot at. He almost certainly had a Glock Model 35, .40 caliber, with fifteen bullets in the standard magazine and several spare clips on his belt. It was highly likely he had an even higher-capacity magazine. He fired at both of us many times. I didn't count, but it was more than ten times. The six-shooter days had been over for a long time. He did not hit me, at least not my soft fleshly part, but one of the bullets hit the bag of quarters on my right side.

Bang! When the bullet hit the bag of quarters, it seemed to explode; the quarters scattered all around me. I was in a silver circle for a split second. The sudden force made me lose my balance and fall on the ground. The quarters had protected me like a coat of mail protected the knights in the Middle Ages. Perhaps I should research making bullet proof vests out of coins. I wonder if the brass pennies would have proved any better than the nickel quarters.

I stood up. It was pitch-dark where I was. My wife had disappeared. I could see the policeman in the beginning of the long driveway, but I knew he couldn't see. I was wearing a black hoodie; my regular "uniform" comes in handy when running from the law in the dark.

I backed up slowly, came to a fence, turned around, and climbed it. Now I was under a magnolia tree, feeling with my hands in front of me, as it was pitch-dark. No moon out tonight. Suddenly, I touched a body. We both jumped but managed to keep quiet. We held hands and tried to make our way out of this backyard. We were behind a three-car garage. We went right till we reached the corner and a fence. There was a two-foot space between the garage and the fence. That was so typical with those rich folks. They wanted to live in big houses, but the developers squeezed as many mansions on their development as possible so that the houses almost butted up to each other. Add to that large garages and pools, and you can pretty much get rid of your lawnmower.

We came around to the front of the garage, where a bicycle was leaning against the garage door. (I wondered if they knew I was coming.) I jumped on it, and my wife got on the little luggage carrier on the back. We rode down the driveway, right passed the homeowners' gazebo-style kitchen window, where a golden retriever with his front paws on the windowsill was barking and wagging his tail. Sorry, buddy, we can't take you for a walk today. Retrievers go home with anybody.

We rode that bike a long ways, ditched it near a bar that was still open, and called a taxi. When the taxi driver arrived, he assumed we'd just come out of the joint and were incapacitated. We did smell like we'd been dancing. We took a ride till we'd arrived about two blocks from our apartment and walked the rest of the way. There hadn't been much loot at the store, and we'd almost got caught. We hoped our partner in crime did not squeal on us.

The policemen ended up asking him a lot of questions at the station. They did keep him in the county jail a few nights. We send somebody to bond him out.

Crime does not pay all the time. This time, it did not; it almost got us caught.

CHAPTER 9

ESCAPE BY FOUR-WHEELER

As I described before, for a few years, I lived at an apartment complex on Beltway 8 called "the Reserves," City Center East. I picked this complex after doing an extended survey of it and many other apartment complexes. I chose this one because of its layout and location. You'll see further into this chapter that it was a proper location for a somewhat paranoid fugitive from the law.

There were fourteen buildings in the shape of two large letter *C*'s, a larger *C* on the outside circling the whole complex and a smaller *C* on the inside, where the administration building, pool, washateria, and such were located. With that layout, there were actually four ways to get in and out of the complex; if one way was blocked, one could always drive through the grass and hit another exit.

To the north of the complex was a high-voltage power line right-of-way (which meant nobody would ever build there). A dirt track frequented by ATVs ran right under the power lines, and a drainage ditch ran alongside it. All that made for a good escape route, either with a four-wheeler or a bike or on foot. If you were very desperate and had to crawl through a drainage ditch, it would take you under roads and sometimes buildings. In a later chapter, I will tell you how I crawled, with my wife, through a ditch, under an unsuspecting police car that was part of a "locked down area," stationed there to prevent my escape.

SWAT team at the front door

This was going to be the last night in my apartment—or the last afternoon, I should say. From experience, I knew the SWAT team usually operates at night, when their dark clothing, training and night vision gives them more of an advantage. Through the rumblings in the underworld grapevine, I'd concluded that, perhaps, somebody had ratted on me, which happens quite often in my line of work. It was either that or, for some other reason—cell phone tracking perhaps, maybe purchases made, or some other way—the law had become aware of my location. And I was slightly on edge, alarmed, restless.

I had made quite a few preparations in case my location was compromised. And sure enough, they decided to raid me on the Fourth of July. Perhaps they were tired of my Independence Day. Perhaps somebody was watching over me to keep my independence intact a little longer.

There was a knock on the door. The fact that the visitor was *already* at the front door set off alarm bells; a person who did *not* live there did *not* have the code to the gate and would have to call you from the front gate, so you could buzz open the gate. I had received no such call and was not expecting visitors that day.

I looked through the fish-eye and saw a police officer. I knew that, from that moment, I wouldn't have much time; flash grenades would soon be thrown through the front window. Well, at least they would try. What they didn't know was that I'd installed thick Plexiglas on the inside of each window, which would prevent a sudden breach, giving me a few more precious seconds.

I gathered my belongings—laptop, money, Krugerrands, cell phone, a few clothes, and my ready-to-run briefcase. And—sorry, neighbors—I started a fire. I kept five gallons of gas at the front door, which I turned over after making a gas trail from the kitchen to the front door, and lit the "fuse" from the kitchen.

This was a strategy I'd learned from the Russians. When Napoleon took over Moscow, he thought he had it made, but the Russians burnt their own city as they retreated, leaving nothing for Napoleon to use. The "scorched-earth policy" was what I also had in mind. Fire would cause so much confusion that my getaway would be an afterthought.

Unbeknownst to anybody, I had rented the apartment connected to my rear wall also, and my carpenter friend, Carrot, had made a hidden door in the wall of the kitchen, between the dishwasher and the sink. This door opened up in exactly the same location in my mirror "safe" apartment. Before I dropped the almost invisible door behind me in my apartment, I threw a match on the gas trail. I dropped the door, crawled to the empty apartment, dropped the door there also, and locked and concealed it. I paused for a minute when I heard a large *boom*. The five-gallon gas tank had exploded right by the front door. Not to worry, the SWAT team had not been able to break through the reinforced door. Nobody got burnt. But they for sure were not able to enter the apartment. And when they finally did, there was nothing to trace back to me.

This made me Houston's Most Wanted. The most efficient way *not* to get caught is to cause as many distractions as possible.

The apartment was now on fire, which made it a lot harder for the police to find me. The fire also set off a fire alarm at the closest city fire station. Firefighters would be here in a few minutes, creating more traffic, along with people consequently starting to run out of their apartments or just coming to see what was burning. All these things created a giant diversion, which allowed for my safe withdrawal from that "hot" location.

The nearest fire station, Houston Fire Station 49, was on 1212 Gesner Rd, about four miles away. Even it was close, the notorious Houston traffic would delay the fire trucks a little bit, even with screaming horns and flashing lights. They would be here in five to ten minutes.

I was living upstairs and knew that the neighbor below me worked the evening shift from 4:00 p.m. till midnight. So, he wouldn't be hurt; he might have some water damage though. I would try to remember to send him a compensation check for $10,000 or something; he had always been nice to me. He had invited me over for coffee and barbeque at times. And after Janet's death, the running and thieving lifestyle was a lonely life. You can't make too many friends when you're constantly breaking the law.

Bang! The SWAT team used a ram on the front door. Access would not be easy, as I'd installed a Titan Steel door (without the apartment manager's knowledge). The door, besides being made of steel, had eighteen bolts (five on each side and four on the top and the bottom) that went into the frame when you locked it and make it nearly impossible to penetrate. It would take them a few minutes to figure out how to break through this front door. It wasn't even for sale here, so they couldn't have practiced on it. I'd ordered it from the United Kingdom. The SWAT team all would be wearing bulletproof vests, but they were not fireproof. I doubted they could make much progress. This would really slow them down, but I still knew I had to hurry.

The empty apartment I'd rented in a fake name was upstairs also. I put on a disguise—a black leather jacket and a Resistol hat, size 7 and 1/2, the Al Capone gangster style. And I walked down the stairs as many neighbors were doing, wondering what had exploded and what was on fire. Everybody was worried about their own thing, go figure.

At the bottom of the stairs, under a silver tarp was a Honda 350 four-wheeler. I'd bought it not too long ago for "such a time as this." It had a snorkel and a big Yeti Tundra 35 cooler tied on the rear rack. The reason I'd bought this slightly taller cooler was, if you have to make a fast run through the woods, you want to be a narrow as possible to make it through the big thicket, which I was about to demonstrate. I put my laptop, and other belongings in the cooler, and strapped it shut with the big black rubber ball ties. Now I knew they would be OK. The Yeti cooler is just as good at keeping water *out* as it is at keeping ice and water *in*. Thank you, guys.

After removing the tarp all the way, I climbed on the Honda four-wheeler and cranked it up. It was camouflaged of course; I was not going to buy a yellow one to make a run for the border, duh. I'd had the mufflers modified so they made minimum sound, in contrast to today's teenagers, who you can hear coming a mile away.

They told me, "If it's too loud, you're too old!' I wasn't really that old, but the SWAT team was a stone's throw away on the other side of the building, and they were heavily armed and would *not* take no for an answer.

I went northwest slowly, trying not to attract any attention. A lot of people were milling around, some hanging out of the balcony, some on the stairs. But I was the only one with a four-wheeler, and I was the only one moving *away* from the scene of the crime.

Usually the SWAT team establishes a perimeter, but in this case, they did not surround the building (their mistake). I guess they figured my apartment only had doors and windows on the front side. Yep, that was true. But they had not factored in the door I'd added.

They did, however, have men positioned at each corner of my building, and I passed not too far from one of them. I don't know if it was my hat or coat or the four-wheeler. Perhaps it was his excellent training. Whatever the case, he was suspicious of me and ordered me to stop.

I ignored the powers that be and floored it. I knew he wouldn't shoot; there were too many people out in the open. He would, however, immediately get on his radio and redirect all his colleagues to where I really was, *not* the burning apartment. I went straight north and took a left turn between two buildings with sixteen apartments each, eight on both sides. I knew I would come out in the resident parking area, where there were covered shelters at the edge of the property and open parking closer to the building.

The Honda rumbled and got me there in five seconds. I didn't know if they had the chopper already active or if it was on call. If the chopper was there, I wouldn't have a chance to escape. But if not (and it wasn't), I had a fair chance to outrun cops on foot and certainly the ones in the cruisers or heavier Suburbans. The route I'd planned certainly was too soft to support any vehicle other than a four-wheeler.

I turned north on the cement and raced toward the edge of the parking area. The entire complex was surrounded by an eight-foot cedar fence. The "gateway" I was about to create for my exit point used to have one treated four-by-four toward the bottom and one toward the top where the cedar boards were attached. I'd removed the one on the bottom a long time ago.

This was also where I parked one of my getaway vehicles—a Ford 150 Lariat bought from the traveling car dealer (more about that in another chapter). The four-by-four was still in the back of the Ford. Yes, they would probably notice. But then, I would most likely be far, far away. And it was an untraceable stolen vehicle anyway, with the keys in the rear bumper. This was my SOP no matter where I lived, one or two vehicles ready to go at any time.

I ran the Honda four-wheeler into the cedar fence at about thirty miles an hour. It fell flat backward and made a way for me to go down into the dry drainage ditch and take an immediate left.

I raced through the grass toward Brittmore Road and went through the large nine-foot-tall corrugated iron culvert. I heard bullets fly past me and hit the concrete pillars of the little overpass; they were shooting at me. That did contribute to a sense of urgency in my escape. I was not bullet proof. But it was starting to get dark, and they were too far away to target me clearly.

After the same distance, about a block through the grass, I made a sharp right turn. There was a steel rebar business on the corner. I followed a dirt path. The only way to get across the road on my left was through another culvert. This one was concrete and four feet across. The four-wheeler barely fit through there. I had walked out here and measured it before.

I'd been running from the cops for so long, the first thing I did when I lived somewhere was plan my escape. What a lifestyle, huh.

I guess I would be well prepared for a zombie outbreak. Except these were not stumbling zombies after me but, rather, highly trained, intelligent law officers.

Their police cars were not able to drive down the same drainage ditch I'd taken. Instead, they came down Kersten Drive; followed it to the left, which was Alcott Drive; and then came down a business driveway. This took them pretty close to where I turned right.

There were no streetlights there, and I'd kept the lights of the four-wheeler off also. They would have to stop their vehicles and turn their engines off to hear me. By this time, I was already halfway under the road through the culvert. I was covered in spider webs and splattered wet from the green algae water that permanently covered the bottom four inches of the culvert. I was concerned that the solid concrete walls of the culvert would act like a sound tunnel on both sides. Many things race through your mind if you're running for your life.

By now, the SWAT team would be headed toward me with their armored vehicle. Where I went, an armored vehicle would be too heavy to make any progress.

When I came out of the culvert, I took a short left and then a right turn onto a dirt road that took me in between two nasty-smelling green holding ponds. I'm not sure if one of the nearby business was allowed to dump there or if the nastiness was from the cattle that used to graze in this area. Somebody had left some cows to graze here.

Not many Houstonians know that there's a fairly large "wilderness area" close to their residences. It's approximately twenty-eight square miles, which is quite large for a city like Houston. You would think it would be built full of skyscrapers by now. However, the area is very low and swampy, and soil tests established it would not be able to sustain large structures without them settling and making the tower of Pisa look like child's play, so it was left undeveloped, except for Bear Creek Park.

Bear Creek Park was carved out of the rest of the swamplands because it was a little higher. There were several pavilions there, which could be used for state fairs and the like; twelve baseball diamonds; four tennis courts; and plenty of room for other family outings. Some of the area was paved parking, but there were many grass parking areas that would allow for plenty of visitors and revenue in the summer months. But I digress.

The twenty-eight acres was bordered by Beltway 8 on the east, Interstate 10 on the south, Baker Cypress Road on the west, and Clay Road on the north (roughly). But I was not concerned with that large area. The part I'd scouted out for a possible escape by four-wheeler was between Beltway 8 and Eldridge Parkway to the east and the west and I-10 and Clay Road to the north and the south, about twelve square miles. Hopefully, it would enough territory to shake my anxious hunters.

After passing the ponds, I was in bush country—many cedars, lots of yaupon bushes, and a few old trails. There were no signs, no pavement, and lots of little and fairly large ponds.

By this time the SWAT vehicle had made its way onto the levy I'd gone under by way of the four-foot concrete culverts. Boy, those guys were faster than I'd thought they'd be. I was the hunted; they were the hunters.

Pfeeeeew. They shot off a flare from a flare gun. At about a thousand feet, it released a bright light that slowly came down on a parachute. If they'd have used their infrared vision, they would have seen the heat signature of my four-wheeler, perhaps a tactical mistake on their part. I wasn't going to stop and remind them.

The swampy area was bathed in light, which didn't really help them that much, as here were so many cedar trees and large yaupons to provide cover for me. I was going straight west, following the advice, "Go west, my son, go west!"

From a distance, I could hear the sound of two or three other four-wheelers. The police had realized they needed to fight fire with fire. But I was way ahead of them.

I swerved around barely visible trees and bushes and splashed through watery areas, some afoot deep, some two feet deep. I could hear the four-wheelers get closer to me.

Branches hit my face and my legs. Believe it or not, I still had that black Resistol hat on. It fitted well, and it was one of my favorite hats. I didn't want to lose it. Certainly, some hairs would give my DNA away.

My goal was to make it straight across the swamp and climb up the levy and cross East Eldridge Parkway, close to the park office. Across Vietnam Memorial Street from the park office was a public parking lot. In the northwest corner of that parking lot, under some trees I had a getaway car parked. Like I said before, I always invested in some cars parked near and far, for such a time as this.

I went through a deep gully and almost lost control. The Honda dropped on its side and lay on my leg. Because the soil was wet and soft, I was able to pull my leg from under the engine and straighten the Honda. I could now see the lights of the four-wheelers headed my direction. There were three, one more toward the north, one toward the south, and one headed straight toward me.

I knew they couldn't see me. I'd removed any kind of reflector or chrome from the Honda and painted some parts with flat black barbeque paint. Still, there was no helicopter buzzing overhead. They must have figured they had enough resources committed to catching Houston's Most Wanted.

At this point, I was so close to North Eldridge Parkway I could see the headlights of the cars going north and south. This was not the location I'd planned to cross over. The road was ten feet above the park at this point. I needed to go north. I turned left.

Suddenly, I crashed about three feet down into a pond. The engine was still running, as I'd installed a snorkel kit with three tubes that protruded higher than the steering wheel and kept oxygen supplied to the engine.

Stunned, I sat there. The engine and seat was completely submerged in the water. My legs were wet, and my shoes filled with water. The four-wheeler did not sink, because the tires gave it quite a bit of buoyancy, and the Yeti cooler provided more floatation to keep my heavy behind from dragging us down.

The four-wheeler of the middle cop approach my location at a great speed. I leaned over the steering wheel, my chest hitting the water and the black hat providing me with shelter to keep my pale face from giving away my location.

The policeman must have seen the pond I landed in. It was about fifty-feet-by-fifty-feet and looked too deep to cross. He sped past me toward the west. I saw the lights of the other four-wheeler to the north of me also approach the curb in the parkway, and he could only go north or south at that point.

Assuming his buddies covered the middle and the south part of the woods, he turned north towards Clay Road. I saw his rear lights disappear between the shrubs and trees.

I was alone, wet—*very* wet but alone. I waited a while, in the quietness. I heard a helicopter far away. If they'd sent the pilot to catch me, I'd better hurry. My body and the exhaust of the Honda would show up as big white spots in those dark woods, and the officers in the helicopter would be able to point the four-wheelers to my exact location.

When I turned the ignition key back on, it made a red light turn on above the gas tank. I kicked the gear shift, which was under water, until it was in neutral, and a green light appeared. The start button sent some juice to the starter, and the engine started purring under water, which made it a little quieter than I would have been above the water; that was a plus. It sounded like a kid blowing bubbles in the bathtub.

The wheels started spinning loose. Floating in the water, they became paddles, and slowly the Honda started to cross the pond. Most of this area was swampy wet, and I was not worried there was a steep bank for me to climb out, and that proved to be true. The water might have been four to six feet deep in the middle, but when I approached the edge, it went from afoot deep to zero in no time.

Back on four wheels, my speed increased dramatically. I could still see in the distance the red light of the police four-wheeler that had turned north. I followed him. As long as he didn't turn around, I was safe. Veering to the left brought me to the edge of North Eldridge Parkway. There were a few places where the park service had entranceways to inspect the park. I came to a steel bar across a dirt trail with posts parked too close together for cars but just wide enough for my four-wheeler to pass through.

After waiting for a lull in traffic, I crossed East Eldridge Parkway, and was able to locate my position because of the slight left curve in the road. My car was parked about six hundred feet south of me location. I turned my lights on. Many cars were passing me on the road as I drove down the median in the grass. Driving without lights in the dark might have raised suspicion from a driver, who then would go on the cell phone and tattletale my position to the authorities.

In about two minutes, I turned right near War Memorial Street; another two hundred feet, and I turned right into the parking lot closest to the four of the baseball diamonds. There was my faithful steed—a black Honda Civic four-door. It had a lot of miles on it, over 200,000. The Civic's reputation for dependability made it an excellent choice for a standby vehicle.

The keys were in the rear bumper with a magnetic key holder. After retrieving them, I undid the Yeti cooler from the four-wheeler and put it in the trunk of the Civic.

Before I drove off in the Civic, I drove the four-wheeler to the "clubhouse." There were the concession stands and bathrooms. I drove right past them and parked the four-wheeler into the bushes as far as I could. It was practically invisible. Then I walked back to the car.

I cranked it up and drove away. I took a left on Vietnam War Memorial Street; a right on East Eldridge Parkway in about two miles; a left on Interstate 10; and, after about three miles on I-10, a right on Beltway 8. I stayed on Beltway 8 one-quarter of the way around Houston, until it crosses with Interstate 45 and then took interstate 45 to Galveston, about an hour drive total.

With that, I left a totally shocked SWAT team nothing but a burning apartment and lost three highly trained professional bounty hunters behind. They were most likely very frustrated, having not apprehended their suspect, though they got very close—front door close actually. I headed to one of my safe houses on Galveston.

The next morning, I dug up some more Krugerrands from my stash and started life over. I had to find a new apartment, a new cover, a new car, and new disguises.

I was getting tired of running, especially alone.

CHAPTER 10

ROBBING THE PRINTSHOP

Most people, when they need a new photocopier, go to Office Depot or Best Buy. My modus operandi was slightly different. I stole one. Well, that's a lie; I stole *many* different kinds of office equipment. Whatever I felt I needed, I apprehended or "organized."

There are a lot of print shops in Houston. I scouted out a few and settled on the one near the Galleria Mall. The mall was on one side of the 610 Loop; this print shop was on the opposite side of the Loop on Vossdale Lane. It was called Springs Printing. The location assured me that most of the traffic and attention would be focused on the mall. When a mall opens, there are a lot of "leech" type businesses that move into that part of town to make opportunity of the increased traffic. Location, location, location, I guess.

This store was surrounded by a concrete parking lot; in the back was a cedar fence, with a residential neighborhood directly behind it. The houses behind the print shop had large trees that blocked the view to the back of the store I intended to rob. It had a lot of glass in the front. The backdoor was a double wide steel door, allowing them to roll the large printing equipment into the facility and allowing me to roll them out quickly. Thanks, Spring Printing. I knew that, if I obtained access to the front, I could leave it securely shut behind me and use the double back door to relieve the shop of some modern office equipment fairly quickly.

Spring Printing had the most advanced copying equipment and printers, which was right up my alley. I like to keep up with the Joneses. They were open from 9:00 a.m. until 9:00 p.m. I parked in the rear parking lot at 2:00 a.m., used a BB gun to shoot out two halogen parking lot lights, and cut the phone lines. (Will security companies ever learn to route their alarms through anything but copper?)

After a short wait, I went to the front, used my lock picking skills to open the front door, and locked it behind me. I could see the alarm control box and recognized the brand as not normally having an internal or external siren. This type of control box routed a signal to the local police station, but since Ma Bell's phone line was interrupted by my sharp wire cutters, no such thing would happen. I would either blatantly refuse it, or turn my head and remove myself from the situation. This had proven to be a very crucial strategy and made it a lot harder for the Houston Police and the FBI to find me. They had no idea what I looked like! When I did make a picture for a false ID card, I used a wig, a mustache, glasses, or any combination of those to hide my true identity.

This cloak-and-dagger approach worked well for my appearance but also for my vehicles.

Stolen item number 1: A printer

I knew Spring Printing had a very unusual printer in this shop. I'd seen the results and was very impressed. It was a Xerox Phaser 8560 color printer. It did not use regular print cartridges but, rather, blocks of colored wax. The printer actually melted the wax and used it as the print medium—the end result being you could actually "feel" the letters on the paper. The resulting quality has no equal in the printing business. I unplugged the printer, tilted it a little bit, and scooted my dolly underneath. It was about a foot and a half square and almost two feet tall. That was not the problem. But the solid construction made this piece of art weigh almost sixty pounds. I promptly rolled it to my truck and loaded it in the back. It was almost too heavy for me to lift up that high. I was getting too old for this.

When you buy this kind of equipment at an office supply store, it's usually in a nice box with handles built in, and one of the clerks is always happy to load it for you. Not so when you steal one; you have to load it all by yourself—bummer.

Stolen item number two: The manager's identity

The manager's office was rather large, with a beautiful L-shaped, shiny red oak desk. The desk was very organized, with black mesh matching letter tray, pencil holder, and letter holder. Behind the desk was a light brown calfskin leather chair. It looked very comfortable. I tried it out, and sure enough, I could just imagine the manager leaning back with his feet on the corner of the desk watching the customers come in and out and the money rolling in.

Sitting in that chair, I couldn't help but stare at the family picture in the corner of the desk. It showed what had to be the store manager with his cute wife and kids. It struck me that he was about my size and build. The desk drawer was locked. I pried it open. Inside the legal-size bottom file folder drawer was a commercial, dark green leather checkbook holder. I opened it up. Inside was a large checkbook with a ledger on the left and preprinted checks on the right.

I took the checkbook and the family picture and went out the back door; it slammed shut behind me. I'd been inside Spring Printing for exactly two hours. Guess how much money I made in one hour of hard work? You'd be amazed.

Driving out of the parking lot, I immediately entered the 610 Loop and drove around Houston once. The fugitive lifestyle I was living is not the most enviable one. I was constantly watching behind me to see if I was followed. The extra driving was one way to find out if I had a tail or not. I drove different speeds, sometimes eighty, sometimes fifty, and looked in my mirrors a lot. I passed cars and let a lot of cars pass me. When no suspicious cars were observed, I was assured of another uninterrupted visit to help myself to some much-needed material possessions.

Stolen item number three: A photocopier

The next thing I stole was a Canon Photocopier, not just any photo copier but a full color one. This one was an Image Runner Advance C3325i; it made very high-quality photocopies. When you go shopping for a new gadget or car or just about anything, it's good to familiarize yourself with the prices and abilities of those products, right? I did the same thing before I organized what I needed. I made a pick list. I had studied the specifications of several different brands and had settled on this one. Spring Printing just happened to have one, slightly used.

This copier had several legal-size paper trays and a large automatic feeder and collator; it could make two sided copies, even in color, and was superfast. It was mounted on a cabinet filled up with reams of paper of different colors and thicknesses, just like they knew I was coming.

All these supplies came in really handy. The copier had its own wheels, but they were just for rolling in the office on vinyl and so on. To transport it safely and securely over the concrete to my truck, I'd brought a dolly. I rolled the copier out the double back door and loaded it in my truck. The dolly had wide rubber straps on the back, which allowed me to pull the copier up the tailgate and set it against the rear window.

Stolen item number 4: A badge / electronic ID creator

Katy Mall had electronic locks and non-contact card readers installed at all the doors. When you waved your ID card close to the reader, the light turned green, and the door was unlocked by the central computer. Information like your ID, access time, and the door used was kept in a database, allowing Mall security to trace back who came in where and when. The mall had an exclusive contract with Spring Printing to supply them with their access cards, as the printshop was in possession of an Avansia card printer.

This printer used retransfer technology with direct-to-card printing designed for high-quality security cards—with the ability to insert a magnetic stripe with the ISO 7811 standard embedded in the back of the ID card. It would print on both sides using dye sublimation on a transparent film. The printed film was then fused to the card using a thermal bonding process for flawless results. It had a built-in flattener that applied pressure on the warm printed card, ensuring a perfectly flat surface. The loading tray held about thirty blank ID cards.

Not only would this printer make ID cards, it could also be used to create almost indistinguishable false drivers licenses; that was my intended purpose. You would think, with that much brain and brawn, that this was a formidable machine, but it was just about eighteen inches tall and a foot square, weighing forty-four pounds, about as much as a sack of deer corn. I carried it to the truck but put it on the back seat and strapped it in. Such a useful piece of equipment needed the royal treatment.

Since the printer supplied ID badges for the Katy Mall, the shop needed a large supply of blank ID cards. I took them also and enough printing supplies to keep me in the false ID business for a few years. This mother lode of supplies would prove to be a very valuable asset to my line of work. I was happy. I was sure the manager would be sad when he walked in in the morning. The print shop's insurance coverage most likely would supply him with an even newer model. Perhaps I should pay them another visit in a month or so.

Before I unplugged the ID / badge maker, I created an Office Max ID card for myself, with a photo of me with black hair and mustache. It came out pretty good. Then I unplugged the device and loaded it into my truck.

Stolen item number five: A magnetic sign printer

To my surprise the printshop had another item that would come in handy—a magnetic sign printer. This Versacamm 540is almost four feet wide and is designed to print on paper or a plastic film. The plastic film is then applied to a magnetic sign.

This Versacamm printer would allow me to make a variety of magnetic signs. When I applied my trade to residential neighborhoods, I could make my approach as "Cook Landscaping" or "Merry Maid Cleaning Services" or "Landry's Air-Conditioning Service." You would be surprised what access you get to backyards or even residences when people see your vehicle with the company logo on both sides.

I tried out the printer and made three Office Max magnetic signs. They came out perfectly. I used these signs and a "hot" white Dodge van to deliver the stolen office supplies to my apartment. When the doorman saw the Office Max signs on the doors of the delivery van, he was convinced it was a delivery for my penthouse. The doors swung wide open. Of course, I was also wearing an Office Max ID card, made at the store before I left.

When I robbed an oral surgeon's house and made several trips to his residence to haul off the loot, my sign said, "Espinoza's Extermination." Nobody bothered me as I walked up the driveway with a mask on. Would you want to get close to me and check out what I was doing and risk breathing poison? Of course not! Magnetic signs come in very handy.

Proper disguise was a necessity for my line of work and something I enjoyed tremendously. In one of my favorite movies, *The Saint*, Val Kilmer uses disguises to avoid being caught. I sometimes modeled my actions after his character.

This is very important! Up until now I had let *nobody* take my picture, not with a camera or a phone. I would not let them.

The 610 Loop around Houston is thirty-eight miles long; driving like I did, it took me an hour to complete the entire circle. Normally I would not have chosen a target so close to my residence, but Springs Printing had the supplies I coveted.

At that time, I was living in the Seven Leaf Tower under a false name, in one of the eight penthouses on the fortieth floor. I called the front desk clerk and told him that, in the morning, I was expecting a shipment of printing supply delivered by Office Max.

I slept a few hours in the van parked at a truck stop.

On my way to my penthouse, I'd called from my cell phone, alerting the doorman that the Office Max van was on its way. Then I put on my Mexican disguise and delivered all the stolen office equipment to my own apartment. The doorkeeper did not recognize me but gave full access without questions asked to me disguised as a Hispanic Office Max employee in a white (stolen) van with magnetic Office Max logos on the front and back doors.

When I arrived and showed him my false ID, he let me deliver all the office equipment to my own apartment without any suspicion. I drove away and later arrived through the basement parking garage in my own car, taking a private elevator to my apartment.

When I arrived home, I went to work quickly, dying my hair black, the same color as the Spring Printing manager's hair. I added a small beard, made a driver's license with my picture and his name on the new ID maker, and left. I first stopped by Texas Optical and bought a set of frames with clear glass in it, matching the glasses the printshop manager wore in the picture on his desk.

At about 10:00 a.m., I arrived at the bank, asked for commercial accounts, and told the clerk I had the opportunity to buy a new property and double the size of my business but that it was currently in the hands of an Indian businessman who only dealt it cash. I wanted to be able to grab this opportunity with both hands, and I needed all the cash I could get my hands on. She took my driver's license and verified I was who I said I was—the rightful owner of Springs Printing.

It took a while for several higher-level employees to make sure I was who I was. They could not call my office, as we were open on Saturday and closed on Mondays. I emptied the bank account, leaving the minimum required $1,000 and walked out with over $500,000 in cash, a suitcase full.

As soon as got in my car, I threw my wig and mustache out the window, still wondering how I'd gotten away with all that and nobody had sounded the alarm. Nobody followed me, and I had "gotten away" with half a million dollars—not bad for about four hours of work. Crime paid that day.

I felt slightly sorry for the poor "pun intended" printshop owner, who came to work the next day and found his copiers and printers missing. Then when he got ready to pay his employees—sorry—he'd discover insufficient funds. I had a nagging feeling; it would take a while to go away.

CHAPTER 11

HOUSES IN THE MILLIONS

It was a beautiful sunny day, the middle of April. It was about seventy-two degrees outside, not a cloud in the sky. Janet and I were driving around Houston on Beltway 8. Suddenly, my eyes were drawn to a billboard that said, "Houses in the Millions." I went, "Hmm," and turned into the subdivision mentioned on that advertisement. It was right past the billboard, the next exit, and not too far from Houston Intercontinental Airport.

I turned into the subdivision and noticed it was designed with one central road and multiple streets leading away and back to the main entrance road, in the shape of a paperclip. The neighborhood reminded me of the location of the Stepford Wives, almost unreal, with fountains and immaculately maintained roses and azalea bushes.

I didn't want to appear too conspicuous. So, before I drove in to the neighborhood, I put some magnetic signs on the door of my truck that said, "Cook Landscaping." I intended to make it "Crook Landscaping" but was afraid my choice of words was too much of a hint, as I really was a crook. My eye fell on a house that was opulent, but something about it made me feel it was unoccupied.

Perhaps it was too clean, too well kept. Usually when people live in a house, they forget something—a shovel, a ball, anything, a telltale that they lived there but were losing it, hee-hee.

Also my criminal "sense" might call it a gift. But who would have been the giver? Hmm. I just had the feeling this house was empty. I parked my "landscaping" pickup in the driveway. I took a rake and shovel out and leaned them against the truck. Now I appeared busy. Have you ever driven by a construction site and seen four or five guys leaning on a shovel. You wonder why the Texas Highways are in such good shape. Not their fault—they didn't do much.

First, I walked to the front door; it was a double-size door with an arch and dark oak, beautiful. In the center of each half was a rosette of stained glass in the shape of a sunflower. Later, we noticed that the flower theme was utilized all through the house. The owners probably used a professional interior designer, who chose the carpet, decorations, colors of the wall, and everything else to impress the neighbors.

There was a round circular window in each door, each similar to the others but not exactly the same. You could tell it was handmade, real glass in lead. The petals were yellow, like the sun; the circle was pale brown and fairly clear. The right door, the one you'd have to open first, had a mail slot in it, brass; it was located about two feet under the stained glass sunflower, about two feet from the ground.

When I peeked through the middle of the sunflower, I could see something. Even though the glass was brown, there was no pattern in it—it was clear—and through that glass I could see a pile of mail behind the front door almost a foot high. The faithful mail carrier had shoved the sales papers, first-class mail, and junk mail faithfully through the mail slot each day, and it made a pretty mountain—a mountain that screamed at me, "Nobody's home. Come and get it!"

My intuition that the occupants were absent was confirmed. Not only was nobody home today; nobody had been home for weeks, months perhaps. I had just become a little bolder; this was the right place, the right time.

We walked to the back of the house. The backyard was fenced with a six-foot cedar fence. The backdoor—which had a two-foot-by-three-foot paned window in it—wasn't visible from the road or the side of the house. The slots "dividing" the glass were between the two layers of glass—a well-insulated door.

From the back door, I could see the alarm system; it looked familiar. When I cupped my hands around my face and held them to the glass, I could take a better look. "*Yes*!" I proclaimed loudly, almost screamed for joy and excitement. I told my wife I knew what brand and type of alarm that was and that it was turned off. She understood that getting caught red-handed was off the table.

I pulled my glass cutter out of my pocket. It was a special one, similar to the compass you drew circles with as a kid in school; but this one had a rubber suction cup on the center post and a glass-cutting wheel on the outside leg. I wetted the suction cup, determined a good location and drew a few hard circles with the diamond cutting wheel. I usually carried an aluminum comb; it could be used as a weapon in an emergency. Here, I used it to tap the mark made by the cutting wheel. The glass popped loose, and the suction cup pulled it out clean. One layer of glass done, the circle cut in the next layer of glass had to be a little smaller for the tool to make a smooth circle.

Attach the suction cup, circle with the diamond, a few taps, and I was in the house—well, at least my right hand was. I was wearing rubber gloves. I didn't not want to leave my calling card. I was sure to make the HPD work hard for it. I unlocked the deadbolt, unlocked the door handle, and swung the door open.

Quite amazing how a ten-dollar tool can get you in a million-dollar house, and boy was this house beautiful. These people had taste. From the front door, you could see a stairway made of glass planks inserted in the wall with lights behind it. When you walked upstairs, it was like walking on light.

My wife and I went to work, swiftly but quietly. First, we made sure we wore rubber gloves and felt shoes around. We did not want to leave tracks or even DNA. We explored the house.

The dining room had a large rosewood oval table that could probably seat ten people. The floor was dark oak, with a large Persian rug. Perfectly sized for this room, it left a little more than a foot around it, where you could see the original floor. It was a little larger than the dining room table. The pattern was peacocks and palm trees. The peacocks were indigo and green; the palm trees were slightly bent, as if they stood in a breeze. I felt the rug with my hand; it felt soft. I found the label in the corner. It was made in Afghanistan out of silk and wool. I could picture the father and his sons sitting in a room with the loom, passing the spindle back and forth and making the thousands of little knots with their hands that attached the tread to the long rolled up cords in a pattern passed on from generation to generations.

And what a contrast that this family living in one of the most restless nations in the world would, in their poverty, create such a thing of beauty that ended up in a peaceful nation with a man who had more money than their country's GNP.

The living room had a fireplace in the middle with four glass sliding doors. Not only was the fire visible from all sides, you could also add firewood from each of the four sides. The bottom and top was brick, but the chimney running from the brick square body to the ceiling was also made of glass. It must have been amazing to stoke this fire in a dark room and see the flames below from wherever you were in the room and to watch them spark and see smoke rising up all the way to the ceiling without causing damage, the heat being contained in fireproof glass.

The library had a large glass reading area built of glass protruding out of the house. The other three walls were books, floor to ceiling, with a ladder that rolled on a steel bar about six feet from the floor and rubber wheels on the bamboo floor. It smelled like a downtown library. There were companies that sold you books by the foot and furnished a library without you ever having to read one book. Conveniences had made us stupid.

The kitchen had an island stove with a JennAir range and black marble top. The black marble on the counters was offset by all the brushed stainless steel appliances, mostly Bosch brand.

We decided to start upstairs. That way, if anybody was walking around the house, we wouldn't be disturbed. There were five bedrooms. We started with the smallest one. We looked through the walk-in closet, checked out all the clothes and boxes there, and felt for hidden walls. We looked under the bed and the mattress. There wasn't much there, except good-quality clothing that could be sold to a secondhand store but was too heavy to carry and not enough return on investment.

The second room had a sign on the door, Victoria. We later found out she was the daughter of the couple who resided there. There was a hope chest under the window. My wife opened it and picked up a light blue shoebox. Inside the shoe box she found a letter, which she started reading. When she was halfway through, she kept saying, "Oh my. Oh my."

I asked her, "What's the matter?"

She read the letter out loud.

Later, we found out the house belonged to an oncologist, and his wife was a pediatrician. She worked for the Houston School District. One of our friend's children had been treated by her; she later diagnosed their daughter with autism. They weren't exactly blue-collar workers.

The letter said:

> Dear Victoria,
>
> We are taking a leave of absence from our jobs and making a trip around the world—something we always wanted to do before we get too old to travel. We are going to see the London Eye, the

> Eiffel Tower, Brussels, the Pyramids, and the Taj Mahal. And any other destination to fit our fancy. We have scheduled groundskeepers, housekeepers, and a friend with the Houston Police Department to keep an eye on the house.
>
> The bills are all on auto pay. Don't worry about that. We expect to be gone a year or more, spending your inheritance. You know that's not true. There will be plenty left over, so don't worry. Should anything happen to us, here is some cash to get you started. The rest of the money is in the safe. You know your dad never trusted banks. There should be close to $2million there.
>
> Our wills and power of attorneys are all up to date. Since your brother passed away, you are our only heir and a very special daughter indeed. We will have our satellite phone, but don't plan to use it much; we plan to immerse ourselves in the cultures of the continents and countries where we are. Email us now and then. Your dad promised he would check on you infrequently. We know you are busy with your job and your new fiancée.

My knees buckled when I heard about the $2 million, right here under our fingertips. All we needed to do was find the safe; opening it wouldn't be too much of a problem. I had plenty of experience there.

I kept thinking over and over about that one sentence: "The rest of the money is in the safe."

The shoebox had $20,000 in cash, which, to us, was proof the letter was valid also. And by the size and opulence of the house and furnishings, we could extrapolate the owners were very wealthy people—people who could afford a yearlong bucket list trip around the world without it hurting their pocketbook.

By looking through the mail, we could also determine their net worth. They had letters from MD Anderson and other hospitals thanking him for his service and asking him to reconsider his temporary absence. In his study was his medical diploma on the wall, with the Hippocratic oath. Same thing for her. She'd received her doctorate from Rice University magna cum laude.

We searched and searched. We looked behind all the paintings and behind *all* the books in the library. We tried to move the fridge and the stove and searched pretty much everywhere. We looked for small Allen screws in the paneling. We checked where the carpet lines changed over to tiles or wood floors—anywhere there would be a chance of finding a hidden hinge. We looked under the Persian rug and under the dining room table. We searched all day.

We searched every room, every nook and cranny meticulously. We went wall to wall, room to room, and corner to corner, checking every piece of furniture to see if it had been moved. We looked for scratches in the floor where hidden doors would have left small telltale signs of a secret room or safe. We found nothing.

The ceiling was Sheetrock, vaulted in some rooms—no secrets there. We found a door that led to the attics by a staircase, where you could see the attic and the insulation. We poked around the insulation, to no use. A safe that could hide that amount of money would fall straight through the ceiling on the owners' head, or at least crack the pretty tile floor.

My guess was there was a hidden door in the library. I lay on my stomach, and it looked like one of the bookshelves had wheels that would allow it to roll forward without making a mark of any kind. We looked behind the air-conditioning intake vent and behind the large full-size mirrors in the bedrooms to see if there was a passage there—nothing!

The wood flooring in some of the rooms had cracks where the boards met, but none of them were in a pattern that could accommodate a safe large enough to hide that kind of money. And the vaulted ceilings in the rooms would not leave much space between the first floor and the second. Usually, in Texas, there is no option to make a basement because of the gumbo mud and flooding, unless you had a way to make it totally waterproof. I only knew of one man who had a basement in his house as a storm shelter, shelves lined with canning jars. It had a sump pump in the corner lower than the floor to keep it from accumulating any water seeping through the walls or floor.

Some people have a hiding place under the stair case. In this house, the staircase was made of glass and open beneath. There wasn't the option there.

Eventually we left, very disappointed and frustrated. We took just the cash, careful not to leave any tracks. We put everything back where it was. I decided to come back the next day with my brother.

My brother, Simon, was in the same trade as I was but not full time. He also worked construction. One time, he helped build a development unit of townhouses with over five hundred units. This was what he did during the building phase. When the townhouses were being constructed, his job was to hang all the doors. The doors had pre-mounted locks and two sets of keys. My brother made copies of all five hundred plus front door keys at the local hardware store, as he was hanging the doors. He tagged all the keys for the townhouses they belonged to. Unbeknown to the developer, he kept them in his possession for years.

Ten years later, we went back and helped ourselves to a lot of stuff; it wasn't breaking an entry, just entry, because we had the keys. We were able to enter the apartments without leaving any trace, take what we wanted, and lock the doors behind us, leaving the owners and HPD baffled.

They never caught on. It was one of the great unsolved mysteries in the Houston crime scene. Who would think back ten years and figure out we had all the keys neatly hanging in a key cabinet, properly labeled and organized. I was very proud of my brother for having the foresight to plan this large-scale robbery. We picked up a lot of nice stuff. Usually, the people in town houses were older, retired, lots of widows; we stole a lot of nice clocks, jewelry, some microwaves, stuff that was easy to pawn. We made quite a bit of play money on the side for several years with this collection of keys. When Simon said, "Let's go!" I usually went.

This time, it was my turn. I asked him to come help me find the safe. He came, but he was very on edge. He never liked my thieving line of work, and the whole time we were in that doctor's house, he sweated. He helped me look for the safe. Simon looked in places I would not think of; he had an unconventional way of looking by poking holes with a probe in the wall everywhere.

I was very uncomfortable with that; it would leave a lot of dust in the house. The housekeeper who was keeping this place clean would notice for sure and call the law. It also left formidable footprints and tracks all through the house as he poked holes, not just in wood paneling but also in Sheetrock.

We were in the front lobby, right inside the front door. I asked him to stop, but he kept on probing the walls. I grabbed his arm. It aggravated him, and he pushed me. I pushed back. He hit me. Now I was angry and started swinging at him.

It turned into a regular fistfight. We landed a few right and left hooks on each other's face and side. For a while, we rolled on the floor and wrestled. He was a little smaller than me and managed to roll out of my grip. While I was still on the floor, he kicked me. That made me very angry. I got up and stormed him like a rhino would.

With all my force, weight, and speed I ran him into the wall. He turned sideways to avoid me, his left shoulder toward me. I hit him so hard his right elbow penetrated the sheetrock, and he screamed.

Through the sheetrock, his elbow actually hit a safe—the safe we were looking for. Our fight was over immediately.

We went from raging mad to ecstatic.

I got my drill and diamond bits and my scope from the truck and went to work on the safe. It took me about two hours to open it. With the drill, I made a porthole to see the brass gears. With the scope I lined up the gears and moved the handle to open. The *click* sounded like music to my ears.

The letter was right. The safe was about three by three feet on the inside, and there were close to two hundred stacks of neatly wrapped hundred-dollar bills (worth $10,000 per stack). It would fill a large duffel bag and a suitcase. I gave Simon a briefcase full, which is all he wanted. He was still sweating from fear and bruised where I'd hit him.

We realized this was our final day at the house. We gathered all out tools. We wiped any spots where fingerprints could have been made and mopped the floor with a wet towel on a broom. He had actually bled on the Sheetrock; we cut that out and took it with us.

We loaded everything in my truck, and I locked the door. Before I locked the door, I set the alarm; you did not have to use a code to arm it. That alarm had a fast exit arming setting.

We drove away. We felt like millionaires, and actually, we were. "Houses in the Millions"—the billboard had not lied to us. Only there was one "House in the Millions" fewer in that part of town now.

CHAPTER 12

MY PENTHOUSE LAIR

After finding four safes in the judge's house, one of them with $1 million in currency, I was able to buy a penthouse in Houston for a little less than a million.

One safe in the judge's house was full of guns, some very old and valuable. In that same safe was a large collection of tourbillion watches. Before that, I didn't know what a tourbillion was. But I discovered there's a large underground market, and it was fairly easy to turn those ill-begotten watches into an honest bank balance. Finding buyers in Oman, Germany, and India proved fairly easy. And watches are easy to ship, disguised as cell phones and the like.

One safe was full of dollar bills, euros and Canadian dollars—totaling a little over $1 million. With the help of a financial specialist, paying him 10 percent commission, the money became "clean," and I was able to purchase the penthouse. Some of those fund managers are whizzes with money, and since all of their transactions are done digitally, they've become masters in money laundering. Another zero here and there, another nine strategically placed, and my loot became a large bank account from which I could easily finance my existence for two decades. If that failed, I always had the gold stash in Galveston Island (coordinates in the back of this book).

Right after purchasing the penthouse, I had some major modifications done, mostly at night, mostly illegal, mostly quietly. I have a dear friend with red hair—everybody called him Carrot—who was an expert craftsman. I met him in prison actually, we were cellmates for a while and become fast friends. He could build pretty much anything out of wood, steel, or stone. He constructed two walls in the penthouse.

First, let me describe the inside of the penthouse (see an illustration in the back of the book).

My penthouse was on the top floor. You'd normally access it by using the elevator from the lobby to my entrance. However, the elevator would only go to this floor if I gave the concierge permission. Otherwise it would stop on the floor below. You could also take one of two stair ways. But walking eighteen floors would certainly be a challenge for most people.

Carrot also made two bulletproof safe rooms with steel plates. But more about that later.

Lobby

You came off the elevator into a lobby, facing another elevator. Toward the north would be the large double doors leading into my home. The doors had also been replaced with copper-plated oak doors. Not only were they beautiful, but copper plated oak is fireproof, soundproof, bulletproof, and almost unbreakable. On the inside of the foyer on each side, Carrot mounted four steel brackets. I had four 4x4 beams that would lay in the brackets—one close to the floor, one at knee level, one at waist level, and one at eye level. This was not a lock you could "pick." It worked in medieval times for the lords of castles, and it would work fine for my castle also.

Living room

Right when you stepped into the door, you would enter the living room. But before you could look out, you have to go left or right around a curved bookcase. This way, when you got off the elevators and opened the front doors, you would look into the back of the bookshelves and find a place to hang your wet coat and leave your umbrella and muddy shoes. This was done for security. Should an undesirable person ever gain entrance to the penthouse, the bookshelf would block the person's immediate view and give me time to go to one of the two hidden rooms or the bulletproof safe room or climb to the roof entrance (which was also installed without authorization). In that safe room was a parasail, a parachute with which I could jump off the roof and fly to safety.

If my visitors were amiable persons, I would invite them in to sit on the sectional couch, looking over the city of Houston toward the north. I tremendously enjoyed sitting on the balcony, sipping a cup of gourmet coffee, and watching the sun sink behind the horizon on the left side. Then the city would turn dark. Well, the natural light would disappear, and you would see the glow of thousands of lights in all directions. But the majesty of the sunset would be in your mind a long time.

The living room had a U-shaped, dark brown leather sectional couch. The living room looked toward the north. On the east and the west walls hung paintings by European masters—Vermeer's *The Concert* and Pieter Brueghel's *The Peasant's Wedding*. Having been in the possession of unique tourbillion watches, some of which only twenty or less were produced, gave me the opportunity to trade with European art dealers, who were able to obtain these painting for me. I felt right at home sitting between such beauty created by masters of the art, while watching the sunset, created by the creator of it all.

On chilly days, I would make a fire in the fireplace in the corner. There was a similar fireplace in the bedroom, but they were connected. You could direct the heat from the living room fireplace to the bedroom. This way, you could enjoy the fire while you were awake in the living room and enjoy the warmth in the bedroom while you were asleep.

Library

To the left of the living room was a library with a sixteen-chair meeting room. This is where I laid out my plans with my colleagues if a job required more than several actors. I had an "Ocean 16" meeting there one time. We planned to hit many ATMs at one time. It was orchestrated from Russia. We were part of the Houston group. The Russians had set the daily limit to "unlimited" on all the debit cards they mailed to us. We spread over the city, emptying many sleeping Houstonian's bank accounts. We kept 50 percent for the danger and the trouble and sent the rest to Russia—in empty Vodka crates actually. We made good use of the library then.

Kitchen

To the left (west) of the library was the dining room and the kitchen. The kitchen had an eight-burner stove. I was not good at cooking, but I enjoyed oriental food and hired an Indonesian woman to cook for me at times—*nasi goreng*, *bami goreng*, *croupouk*, and all kinds of flavorful dishes. And other times I had an Indian woman cook for me. She would really be creative. She shopped at Fiesta and made the most palatable curry dishes, not hot but a delight to all the taste buds on your tongue and mouth.

The kitchen had a large pantry, many cabinets under the counters with deep drawers, and many cabinets above the black marble countertop.

Secret equipment room

South of the kitchen, Carrot had blocked off the old door, covered it up with Sheetrock and matched the Sheetrock pattern exactly. The only entrance to the secret room was through the "E" on the floor plan. Along with being a secret entrance to the hidden equipment room, this E also had steel steps bolted into the wall, through which you had access to the room. If the building owners knew about my slight modification, they probably would have cancelled my occupancy.

But they never found out. Carrot had used a concrete cutter and made two holes in the roof of the penthouse, through which I could escape. If the house were to become unsafe—because of either the law or the outlaws wanting to poke holes in me with 9mm slugs, then I would jump into the secret exit, strap on a parachute, climb to the roof, and make a base jump. There were two cars waiting for me with keys ready to take me back to Galveston and start over.

The secret room was loaded with equipment that were tools of the trade for me—a photocopier, a badge / electronic ID creator, a magnetic sign printer, a printer, a computer, a router, an overhead projector, an extra-large monitor, a TV hooked up to cable and local antenna, a typewriter, a paper cutter, a cross shredder, an oven, a vacuum press, a passport camera and printer, a scanner, and do on.

With that equipment, I could make *any* sort of ID as long as I had an original or even a copy or a photograph of the ID. With Photoshop, Paint, and other software, I could create any ID or entrance badge for pretty much any building in Houston.

The safe printer room had a *large* printer (using solid cartridges). All of the equipment in the room was hooked up to the LAN. I could walk all around my house with my smartphone and print anything I could see on my phone. There was a wireless antenna in each room, centered in the ceiling, made invisible either by the smoke detectors or the existing lights.

On the desk on the right was an HP server, different scanners, an old flatbed scanner, and page scanners with the lens located directly above the documents. They might be vintage equipment, but to make certain documents or fake badges, you had to manipulate images and text just the right way. A badge should *not* look perfect;

they never do. I even had a typewriter because some forms actually contained typing, and the typewriter made it look very authentic.

On the table across the room, the one by the two large windows was my cutting and pasting equipment. If you could not manipulate images and text digitally, you sometimes had to cut and paste it the old way. This also gave you the opportunity to create smudges and scratches to make a badge look worn and older, instead of brand new, giving it further proof of authenticity. To do that, I had to have a lot of natural light; that was why I placed my worktable so I had plenty of light and a good view of downtown Houston, my work area. I had to keep my target area in perspective while I created the tools to harvest.

Playroom

To the east of the living room was a very large "playroom." It had a ping-pong table, a pool table, and a foosball game. Against the wall were two old arcade game machines, *Galaga* and *Mrs. Pacman*. I shot golf balls, sometimes from the balcony and, occasionally, from the roof, toward the park. But don't tell anybody that. I hope I never hit a car or a person. These were just a few games to keep my mind off criminal activities like planning my next strike.

Bedroom

To the east of the playroom was the bedroom. There were three east-facing windows. I loved lying in bed and seeing the sun come up. There were no curtains; nobody was high enough around us to look in anyway. But I had Carrot install a large electric roll up screen that covered all three windows and a monitor mounted in the ceiling. So if, before dozing off, I wanted to watch a movie, it would come alive on a seven-by-twelve-foot reflecting screen instead of a monitor. I could make the bedroom pitch-dark with a remote control.

Only the library, the living room and the playroom had access to the balcony by ceiling to floor-sliding windows. But I had Carrot make a door in the corner of the dining room and the bedroom, so that, from every room, I had access to the balcony. That way, I could either make my escape from the balcony or make an invisible switch to the other side of the house and use the emergency roof exit for my getaway. (Horrible to always be on the run, isn't it?)

The bedroom had a large Jacuzzi and a very large walk-in closet, with a side for male and female if need be. It also had two sinks and two showers, with a panel that could be removed to make one large shower. It is much more fun to shower together.

I lived in the penthouse mostly alone, though, and during that time of my life, I liked it that way. My wife had died after the judge's house job, and I missed her dearly. I wasn't ready for another relationship, even though somebody close to me asked to be that special person. I rejected her and felt sorry for years. At that time, I was not ready to give up my easy-living life of crime.

Walk-in closet

In the walk-in closet, hidden right in the middle, was the second emergency exit. This one was similar to the one in the equipment room. You could either go to the disguise room, or you could grab a parachute, climb up to the roof, and "fly" to safety.

Disguise room

I was inspired to make this room after watching the movie *The Saint*. I realized that, in a time of escape, even when the law was close, a proper, instant disguise would be an easy way to make it to safety. Even security cameras wouldn't help in securing your arrest. From a make-up artist, I learned how to plaster up my face, what kind of wig to use, and how to put together all kinds of outfits. Some clothes where starched and clean, some flamboyant and colorful, and others were old and dirty. In this room was a vacuum machine. This way, I could take the clothes with me in minimum space. I could change outfits in a minute and discard whatever I'd been wearing.

This house was my home for about five years. I was able to sell it with a 50 percent profit on the real estate market. First, I had Carrot, my genius contractor, undo all the modifications a square citizen would not need and restore the penthouse to its mostly original condition. The roof modifications were so hidden and so radical they couldn't and wouldn't have to be undone.

After the sale of the penthouse, I was able to buy a Best Western Hotel in Houston for $5 million. You would be amazed how big a loan you can get if you can pay $1 million down. And after hiring a proper management firm, I was able to clip coupons from that investment for many years, securing a retirement fund normally not included in a life of crime.

The hotel made money hand over fist. Not only do you get a steady cash flow when you rent out the rooms, the hotel also increases in value every year. And with *one* night manager, a few maids, and one maintenance man, the income is tremendous and the expenses are minimum. Easy in, hard out is the way to make money with a hotel. I could always find a qualified hotel manager from India to run the hotel efficiently and honestly. The hotel was paid for in five years. We'll leave the light on for you. And I always had a room if I wanted one.

CHAPTER 13

ONE INCH FROM DEATH

Life in the fast lane is a lot faster if you own a bike, and I have owned a few. Not only can you get away faster than most police cars, you can also go through gates and narrow passageways they're not allowed to follow you down. This chapter details some of my escapades where the two-wheeled motorcycle outdid the Crown Victoria with turbocharged engine fairly easily.

A brush with life

This is not really a police escape, but this happened and made me consider my lifestyle. It should have killed me, and I was not ready to die.

It was a hazy Monday morning in September, about seventy-five degrees, 6:00 a.m. I was cruising on my Kawasaki Ninja, going about ninety-five miles per hour down Highway 105. There were only two lanes. Visibility was about twenty feet. Going as fast as I was going, I would never have had time to stop if a vehicle in front of me was turning. So I figured, I'd just drive on the white line in the middle. There were no cat's-eyes in the middle of the road, which made for a smooth ride. Just the slightly roughened surface of the stripes in the center of the road created a slight buzz when the tires rolled over them. Over the sound of the engine, I could hear *fzzzz, fzzzz, fzzzz* in quick succession as I raced in the center of the road.

There were not very many houses there, large fields in between the few structures that were there, and not very many trees in that area either. Unbeknownst to me, a group of deer was crossing that road. And hearing the roar my Kawasaki Ninja's muffler approaching in the fog startled them. They could not hear exactly where I was coming from; their noses, which they use to detect hunters or other danger, were not a useful tool, unless they could smell the slight oil leak in my gearbox. They froze.

I was completely oblivious to the fact that deer would even travel through this area. I especially had no inkling that they would stop in the middle of the road and just stand there. If the visibility had been normal, I would have seen the animals, hit my brakes, and swerved to avoid them. But there was thick fog. I couldn't see them, and they couldn't see me as I barreled toward them at ninety-five miles per hour.

My hands were on the outer edge of the handgrips. I like to ride this way because it relaxes your hands and prevents them from gripping the handlebars the same all the time. By thus releasing the tension, you avoid cramps in the big muscle in the palm of your hand.

This is how I drilled my way through a standing pack of deer. They never moved. I was only in their presence for 1.3 seconds, but what happened was most amazing.

As I drove through the pack of deer, I could feel them. Both my left pinky knuckle and my right pinky knuckle brushed against a deer. I could feel the hair on their skin rub me. *Wow*!

One inch more to the right or one inch more to the left, and I would have hit a deer with one-hand control and just totally spun out.

My speed and the weight of any deer would have caused some serious damage to me and the deer. It would have flipped me, cart wheeling over the cement. I was wearing yellow tinted sunglasses to cut back on the glare, but I was not wearing a helmet, just a bandana. I doubt I would have survived that impact.

Many times, I thought about that brush with the two deer and how I was spared. *Why was I spared?* I often thought. That was my first near-death experience, one of many.

A narrow ledge stopped the bullet

If you steal, you often end up with things you don't need. They have value but not to you, which makes it imperative that you find somebody who *does* need it—or thinks he does. You have to hustle, and hustling was something I was good at. It was in my blood, and I loved doing it.

I ended up with so much stuff to sell that, one day, I was making a deal at a friend's house to sell him a storage compartment full. He'd already checked out the contents, and we were bickering over the price (or bargaining) when a truck drove by his mobile home.

It had a deep roar—that is, the sound a big engine with a modified muffler would make. It was a *deep* roar—*vroooooom.*

The first time it drove by his house, we didn't pay it any mind. The second time, *vroooooom*, we perked up a little bit. But when it drove off, we went back to doing business. The third time it came by, *vroom*, short, and it suddenly stopped. Then a bunch of bees started flying through his walls; that's what it sounded like.

But what was actually happening was the guy outside started spraying the mobile home with a machine gun. Later, we counted over two hundred bullet holes in the aluminum siding.

We were inside and dropped on the floor. Bullets were flying over our heads and beside us.

One guy had run into the bathroom. It was kind of stupid. But what you do in a situation like this is, sometimes, you make stupid split-second decisions.

When the shooting stopped and the heavy-duty truck sped off with a high volume *vroooooom vroom*, he came back out of the bathroom—with his hand on his chest—saying, "I've been shot!"

He certainly was shot. When he moved his hand away from his chest, that became very obvious. If he didn't get help very quickly, he would faint and worse.

We rushed him to his car and told his buddy to drive him to the hospital and make up a story that he'd been shot while cleaning his pistol. We went back into the house in case the shooter decided to come back.

As soon as we locked the door, his buddy knocked on the door. "The car won't start!"

We ran out there and gave him a jump. All the while the guy who was shot had to hold his hand on the wound. We hoped he would make it.

When the shooting started, I hit the deck. I laid on the floor close to an air-conditioning vent. A square piece of metal stuck out from the wall about half an inch; it was where you'd install a new filter for the AC unit. I was lying right next to that, and a bullet had hit that metal frame about four inches from the floor. I heard the bullet hit; some of the metal and paint splashed in my face.

If that bullet would have entered the mobile home one inch to the left, it would have hit me in the face and traveled to my back and maybe my spine.

I often wondered why I was spared. I had been an inch from death when I'd driven through that flock of deer touching the hair with both my knuckles on the steering wheel. And now again, death was an inch away, this time in the form of a bullet.

I didn't always drive fancy new cars. My cars were stolen and not always in very good shape and or well maintained.

One time, my wife and I went to Mexico on vacation. I had a full set of fake passports and driver's licenses. My skin turned really dark in the summer. I painted my hair black and took on the name Oscar

Montenegro. My wife already had black hair and a dark complexion; she easily could pass for a Mexican lady.

We were in the mountains when my car broke down, far from civilization. We stood at the side of the road for a while. It was a quiet dirt road. Finally, a man came by with a one-ton flatbed truck. He didn't speak any English, and our Spanish was just enough to let him know we needed help—truck, broke! He seemed to indicate he couldn't fix it himself, but in the valley below, he knew somebody who could.

He wrapped a chain around the front bumper of our Toyota ban, attached it to the rear tow hook of his truck, and started racing down the mountainside. What I mean is he could have just driven fifty miles per hour. The mountainside was on the left, the valley on the right, and he drove like a maniac, almost like he'd totally forgotten about us. He was going at least eighty miles per hour! I had no control at all, except the steering wheel; my power brakes did not work. No AC or wipers.

There was only a ten-foot chain between our front bumper and his rear bumper, and when he slowed down to go through one of the hairpin curves, it appeared we were going to run our radiator into his tow hook. But every time, right when irreplaceable damage would have been done to our car, he sped back up, narrowly avoiding a collision.

We were being pulled into oblivion it felt like. I told my wife, "You might as well get down on the floorboard, because we are going to die!"

This is life, I mused later. Things come at you like a tow truck, hauling you down the mountain of life, with divorce, financial problems, health issues, or anything else you have to battle, and there appears nothing you can do about. And often, you also have no control over the final outcome. You really don't think you're going to survive this trial. But you are. Just trust.

In prison, I saw the Crips guy trying to kill a La eMe member, and I just happened to intervene, which brought me millions actually. Why was I spared?

Once I was driving on Beltway 8 and a car was in the lane on my right. In front of that car was a truck loaded with pallets. One pallet fell off. The driver of that ca ran square over it. *All* her tires blew out. She had four flats tires at once, traffic roaring past her. Why did it happen to her and not to me?

So many times in my life, I could have, perhaps should have, been killed. But it seems like I was always spared. I often wondered why. Was there some big play that was still going to unfold, in which I had a role?

CHAPTER 14

CRAWLING THROUGH THE POOP

This is a chapter I'm not particularly fond of writing. It's downright embarrassing. It started all wrong and ended all messy.

Usually, among all the vehicles I owned at any given time, there was a motorcycle or two. One of them was a Honda Magna 1300. It was fairly small but had large engine and was easy to maneuver—a city cruiser.

All of what unfolded was against my MO and came about as a dare, perhaps a marijuana-induced dare—not my smoking, but Janet's. After a joint or two, she wanted to do something we'd never done before.

She said, "Let's get some quick cash from restaurants." And like Adam taking the fruit, I complied. I should have talked her out of it, but I loved her. Love can be blind *and* stupid.

I knew where there were quite a few restaurants in a close proximity.

We jumped on the bike with the only tool in our possession being a two-pound fiberglass hammer and my backpack.

It was 3:00 a.m., when most people are counting sheep. Janet put on her Daisy Dukes and hopped on the back of the bike and said, "Let's go!" almost a girlish excitement in her voice.

Carrabinara's (3:00 a.m.)

We drove to Carrabinara's, on the corner of North Voss Road and Woodway Drive, parked the bike right at the front door, beat our way through the glass, ran to the cash registers, grabbed as much money was we could, and ran back to the bike.

This was probably the stupidest thing I'd ever done. We set off alarms, we were filmed by security cameras, and silent alarms summoned the cops. But we were in love. Don't try this at home.

Buffalo Jack Grill (3:26 a.m.)

We hopped back on the bike and rode to Buffalo Jack Grill on Woodway Lane. Same stupidity. Why I continued doing this while a thousand alarms were going off at the police station and in my mind, I don't honestly know.

We knocked our way through the glass doors, ran to the registers, and actually harvested a large wad of hundred-dollar bills and twenties, almost worth the trouble.

Back on the bike, adrenaline flowing, we could hear the cops headed for Carrabba's.

Submarine Subs (3:58 a.m.)

We sped through the alleyway to Submarine Subs next door. *Bang*, another glass door. The yellow fiberglass hammer did practical work as a rudimentary key. Never knew that the blacksmith hammer with the two-pound head I'd bought at the hardware store recently for $94.04 would come in so handy. Submarine Subs had no money in the cash registers, but the small three-foot square manager's office had many neatly rolled rolls of quarters. My backpack was halfway filled. We weren't getting rich, but we might be close to getting caught.

El Toro Enchilada Kitchen (4:19 a.m.)

At the other end of the parking lot was El Toro Enchilada Kitchen, on the corner of Wood Hollow Lane and Winrock Drive. I had lunch there once; the food was good, and the people were friendly. And this was the thanks I gave them for good service. I robbed them. Low-end scum like me should be in prison, right. Well, maybe later, but we had one more restaurant to go after this one. No money at El Toro, go figure. A mom-and-pop restaurant most likely has the habit of Mom taking all the money home or Pop putting it in the bank.

Piscalante's (4:45 a.m.)

After robbing El Toro Kitchen of nothing but a few mints, I turned the bike left on Winrock and left on Woodway Road—*another* stupid thing. I went back the way we'd come, toward the police sirens. From police headquarters, they could probably see we were on a roll. No telling how many cops cars would be on their way circling the neighborhood. But I knew that Piscalante's was more upscale—more expensive food, more affluent clientele, more money. We were there in three minutes. I parked on the north side, the main entrance, under the canopy in the dark. It was 4:45 a.m. now.

Janet squealed when we obtained entrance through the double glass door, busted with the two-pound hammer. What was wrong with her? If I didn't love her so much I would have traded her for a newer, quieter model.

Upscale restaurants don't keep their money in the cash registers but, rather, in the safe. The manager's office was easy to find. It had a big "Manager" plaque on the front door. The safe was in the corner, four feet high and four feet wide. As it happens, I'd studied its brand and make in prison and knew how to open it. It took me five minutes. The safe was not a problem, but I could not keep Janet from giggling.

There was about $80,000 in the safe. That was a stack about four inches tall for you math geeks. It fit easily in my backpack, which I closed tightly and strapped on my back. I did not bother with the twenties and the smaller bills.

I grabbed Janet. We ran outside, jumped on the Magna, and went north.

We were spotted by a policeman. They had the habit of tattling on their radio. And within five minutes, they had set up a perimeter covering South Voss to the west, Woodway to the south, and South Ripple Creek to the east. North was Buffalo Bayou, and it had rained the night before; it was too full to cross.

We rode north through the three parking lots of the Third Baptist Church campus. After that, I went to the east side of the Bleakwood Nursing Center. We said goodbye to the bike and let it roll of the embankment into Buffalo Bayou. They would find it in the dry season, three months from now.

We proceeded on foot, turning left between the nursing home and the bayou. It was 5:00 a.m.; all the old people would be asleep. Their windows were facing north, most curtains were closed, and most lights were off. Toward the entrance, we could see the security guard in his office, smoking and playing solitaire. It's amazing what a time-wasting practice solitaire actually is—much more fun with real cards.

We saw the cop car on the overpass on North Voss Road where it crossed Buffalo Bayou; he was looking in our direction. It was still dark but starting to get light.

You'd never guess what happened next.

A fog rolled in.

At first, it came from the Bayou, but then it spread through the neighborhoods, encircling the nursing home where we were standing, and under the overpass where the cop was sitting. The fog, however, stayed low, about two feet above the ground. When we were standing, we could not see our feet. So my military training kicked in, and I said, "Let's crawl."

Janet, always the obedient one, had no problem with this. We realized the seriousness of our predicament and that her anxiety and giddiness could get us caught.

We crawled on our bellies from the front entrance of the Bleakwood Nursing Center, right under the nose of the police car, following the bayou grass side; the fog his us from his piercing, hunting eyes.

It was our way through freedom, but there was a stinky side effect of this escape.

The people in the nursing home, it seemed, were allowed to keep pets, and this was where they walked their dogs. We were literally crawling on our bellies through dog feces. And we had to keep going. We had to stay low until we got all the way to the other side of the divided road overpass.

That was a lot of dog mess, and quite a bit of it was rubbed into our shirts, our pants, Janet's knees, and the tips of our shoes. We stank like pigs.

When we were far away from the overpass and we were sure we could not be spotted, we just kept on walking, following the bayou.

We walked hand in hand, all the way to Wickdale Lane, followed it to Memorial, and called a taxi.

I bet that driver had to shampoo his carpet and fumigate his ride before he picked up anybody else.

If it wasn't for my fake nose and mustache, the pictures taken by the security cameras would have actually helped the cops. But as it turned out, sorry, guys

We didn't let the taxi driver take us all the way to our apartment; we never did. We walked the last five blocks home—hand in hand. Janet apologized. I accepted. We went home, threw all our clothes in the dumpster, and took a shower together.

We were in love.

CHAPTER 15

THE TRAVELING CAR LOT

This chapter is about something that is happening in Houston every day, right under your noses, hidden in plain sight, a fact well known to the Houston underworld. The police know, but until now law enforcement has been unable to shut it down. Most likely, that inability is due to supply and demand—the demand is high, and the supply is plentiful.

In a previous chapter, I described how I robbed a delivery service and their drop boxes. I told you how, in one of those drop boxes, I discovered an overnight envelope with a vehicle remote control.

The Houston resident, with his wife and kids, had gone to see Grandma and Grandpa in Florida in their Suburban. Dad had the keys to his Beemer in his pocket, which he left on the nightstand in Grandpa's house in Florida. When they got back to Houston and realized he'd left the Beemer keys, he called his parents and said, "Please send them back to me overnight. I need those keys ASAP to drive to work."

Kind Grandpa sends the keys back overnight, but they do not quite make it all the way to their intended destination. They make it as far as the drop box on the corner of the family's street. That was where I, with the stolen key, emptied the contents of the drop box. I was not very discriminatory concerning what I stole; if it seemed of any importance or value to me, I took it.

This included credit cards, credit card offers, driver's licenses, and passports. It seems idiotic to send passports in such an unprotected manner, as much as foreigners would like to get their hands on one. But they came in quite handy. For one, I could use the ones that looked a little bit like me to put on a disguise and travel abroad under another "clean" name.

In addition, I sold many of those passports the black market. Do you know how much money you can get for a clear new passport? Three grand. Nice paycheck for a few minutes of work.

But I digress.

In one of my hunts, I pulled an overnight envelope out of a box. It had a little bulge in the envelope. Sure enough, it was a remote and key to a BMW.

A clean, fairly new BMW fetches a high price on the black market. On the front of the envelope was an address. Guess what? *That* was the address where the treasure could be found. Easy as pie.

The next night, around 3:00a.m., my darling wife, Janet, drove me a few houses away from the location of my new car. I walked over to the silver four-door BMW sitting in the driveway, just waiting for its new owner. When I was two feet away, I punched the unlock key. Beep. Driver door unlocked. The odd key was really just a square piece of plastic that fit into a square hole and then turned.

The chip in the key, talked to the chip in the car. "Daddy, I'm home." The car cranked with a sweet humming sound. I left the lights off, backed out of the driveway, and turned toward Janet. And off we drove. To where?

To the traveling car lot!

I know you've heard of *The Sisterhood of the Traveling Pants*. Well, this is similar but bigger. You could call it, "Brotherhood of the Traveling Car Lot!"

Have you often wondered what happens to all the cars that get stolen in Houston each year? Easy. They get sold and resold, quickly, sometimes the same night, traded with another out-of-state car.

Have you seen those guys on the highway, usually two cars behind each other, each of them pulling a vehicle behind them? They're usually traveling at night. It's never a family, no wife, no kids, just two shady folks driving four stolen cars. That's how the traveling car lots are supplied. Atlanta, Houston, Chicago, New York City, they're everywhere.

The car lot is only in the same location *one* night. Sometimes, it's downtown in the parking lot of a bank. The next night, it will be in a large grocery store parking lot. The next night it might be south of Beltway8. But will *never* be in the same location two days in a row.

Often, there are fifty cars, most of them less than a year old. There are some older vans and pickup trucks. They're in the abandonment side of the parking lot—meaning you can commit a bank robbery with one of these cars, use it as an escape vehicle, and then park it somewhere or burn it and switch to another stolen car that gets you farther away from the crime scene. That way, your *first* getaway vehicle can't be traced back to you. Just remember to follow the speed limit and don't get pulled over like McVeigh.

The only way to find out where the traveling parking lot is that night is through trusted informants.

They *do* need your business. They know who their faithful suppliers, like me, are—suppliers who often have a stolen car for sale.

Face it, every car lot needs an incoming inventory.

Every transaction is quick—little haggling, cash only. "Bye. Here's the money. Give me the keys."

That night, the car lot was located in the parking garage of a famous shopping mall in northeast Houston. The lot operators liked to hide in plain sight. *No*, not all the cars were on the same floor. They were in designated parking spaces, spread over the entire garage.

A prospective buyer, upon entrance into the parking lot, would be handed a flyer that appeared to be a cake sale with prices. But actually, it was a listing of all the floors and parking spots.

How you bought a car at the traveling car lot

You took a flyer, slowly circled the parking lot floors, going higher and higher. Any car you liked, you marked. Let's say you just wanted one car—a Nissan Rogue, for example. You would drive by slowly and observe the car. You'd keep on circling to the top floor.

There you'd talk to the car lot manager, whose name was not known. Agree on a price, hand him the cash, and you get a key. You circle back to the car. Stop. Let your buddy out. He gets in and drives the car off the lot.

The guard at the gate is in on it. He is paid off with a $5,000 bonus—more than he makes in a month. He raises the beam, and you're free to go. That's how you bought a car.

How you sold a car at the traveling car lot

Selling is very similar. I checked the BMW. It had plenty of gas. I set the GPS to the shopping center of the night. It was about thirty minutes away. Traffic wasn't too bad in Houston at 3:30 a.m.

I drove into the parking lot and grabbed a ticket. If you're wondering how I didn't get my picture taken all these years, I always carried some disguises with me—a wig, a hat, a mustache, and even makeup to turn my skin another shade.

Thanks to body sprays, where a woman steps into to a beauty shop and has her body painted like a Mustang in a paint shop, there were plenty of body paints out there. I used almost every shade. I was a shady person, right?

I circled all the way to the top, showed the BMW to the buyer, and agreed on a price. I asked $7,000 for this one and got it easily.

The manager handed me the cash, and I gave him the keys. He whizzed it off and disabled the On-Star.

Once the hot car you brought is out of your hands, you get in the vehicle with your buddy and head on home.

That's how easy it was to sell a car. No title transfer, no sales tax, no bill of sale, just an exchange of money and keys.

Over the years of being Houston's Most Wanted, I probably supplied the traveling car lot with close to a hundred cars. I might have bought fifty. Usually, I would sell the new ones and buy the clunkers.

It was my MO to keep two vehicles stashed as getaway cars everywhere I lived with magnetic key holders in the rear bumper.

One of the two would often be the vehicle of last resort—the one that got me back to Galveston, to my safe house, and to my stashed gold.

Often, I would park the vehicle in a church parking lot, in the far corner under a tree if I could. One time, at night, I drove an old Ford F-150 of the docks, windows open; it went under in no time. Yes, I did jump out first.

But I felt bad about that, polluting the beautiful bay with a few gallons of gasoline and oil. I never did it again.

CHAPTER 16

ARREST AND TRIAL

Warning: This chapter contains some acts of violence. This is not a violent book. If you want to read about gore, find another book. I never killed anybody. I never committed armed robbery. I never assaulted anybody. My crime of passion was theft, obtaining items by locating and "organizing" them. I lived the lifestyle of the rich and infamous without ever working a job. I was Houston's most wanted thief.

The not-so-pleasant prison journey usually happens in this order:

- You get arrested, no longer a free man.
- You're put in the county jail, no telling how long.
- You go to trial and are sentenced in front of a judge and/or jury.
- You are processed *in*to the Texas Prison System, through the Wall Unit usually.
- You are transported to a prison. (If you have committed a federal crime, you do your state time first, and then you do federal time.)

- You are processed *out* of the Texas Department of Correction, usually through the Wall Unit.
- You probably are going to a halfway house.
- If you get out on parole, you visit your parole officer frequently.
- Then you are a free man again.

Arrested

It all starts with your arrest, which is a very uncomfortable situation—guns pointed at you, cops shouting at you, and so on. I spent quite a few years in prison, not all at once, and I was arrested several times.

I will describe one of the more eventful arrests.

Besides owning a few cars, some of them stashed in different locations, I always owned at least one motorcycle also. They were good for smaller jobs or getting down small alleys or making a getaway when you're in a pinch.

This beautiful sunny Texas day, I was riding my motorcycle through downtown Houston. It was a Kawasaki Police 1000. A friend of mine bought it online from a guy in California, on eBay. He never saw it, never started it, just looked at the pictures, saw what he liked, believed the seller, and ordered it. The deliverers dropped it off in his front yard by truck, and when he got tired of it, I paid cash for it. I never transferred the title, just kept stolen plates on it all the time.

It was a 1000cc straight 4, I figured if the California Police had them, they must be fast, and it was. Chain drive, light weight, still had the metal box on the back that normally had the blue flashing light mounted on it.

Sometimes, I did scare my friends when I drove up with a white and black helmet; it made them nervous. It wasn't at all that I wanted to impersonate the police. I just didn't want them to catch me. Well, it did not help.

Sometimes, I used the bike to scout out neighborhoods. One time, I used it to safely get my wife back (more about that in another chapter). This time, I was headed to a friend's house. I decided to go through downtown Houston to avoid the jammed freeways. Interstate 10 and Interstate 45 go straight through downtown Houston and bring a lot of anxious drivers there.

It makes these highways the biggest parking lot in the world at times, full of screaming people. The laws in Texas aren't the same as those in California. In California, when there's a traffic jam, the motorcycles are allowed to ride between the cars and go to the front of the line. Not in Texas. I guess they're too afraid an opening car door will knock you off the bike. That means that, even on a bike, when there's a traffic jam, you get just as stuck as they are.

A few close calls made me believe the downtown streets would be safer, and they were. But this time, too safe maybe. The "to protect and to serve" gang felt that Houston had to be protected from me, and rightfully so.

Even though I did not let anybody take my picture, one time, an undercover stake out had been able to catch me with a telephoto lens, which gave them some idea of who to look for. And on this wonderful sunny day, I was riding my Kawasaki in downtown Houston. It was hot. I raised my smoke face shield to get some air—shouldn't have—and a policeman got a glimpse of me. He followed me for a few blocks, and then he turned his lights on. Whoop, Whoop. You probably don't know what kind of fear that put in my heart.

I gassed it, hoping my speed and ability to go down narrow streets gave me the edge. It did, but radio signals travel so much faster. I went down Franklin Street, going eighty miles an hour. That was fine, but when I jumped over a railroad track, I became airborne. My wheel was on free spin, and my adrenaline had the throttle all the way down; my RPMs went way over the red line, and my engine blew up. When I heard the metallic clanging and grinding in the engine, I knew it was over.

The rod knocked a hole in the block, and everything jammed; it landed like a lead balloon. I had been about three feet in the air, and when I came down with a locked wheel, it threw me out of balance and the bike fell over on my leg and pinned me down—luckily to the left side, not the right side where the muffler was, or I would have been severely burnt.

Within one minute I was surrounded by cop cars. At first I had my leg stuck under the bike, but I was able to wiggle it loose. There were guns pointed at me from all directions. The cops shouted at me.

"*Get up.*"

"*Stay down.*"

"*Get your hands up in the air.*"

I slowly stood up and told them, "If you guys figure out who your spokesman is and what you want me to do, I will do it."

They approached from several directions with their pistols trained on me; I was not going to move. An ex Houston policeman told me that, at one time, he was looking forward to going to work to get to kill somebody. That was when he got out; he's a truck driver now—can live with his conscience. I did not want to be killed that day and moved slowly and obeyed what I was told.

They got me.

Every time this happened, I breathed a sigh of relief. Living a running life is hard, very hard.

I was slammed against a police car, read my Miranda rights while the handcuffs were placed on me, and somewhat roughly put in the back of a police car. A wrecker was called to pick up the motorcycle. A bike is easy to hide. Park it anywhere with a motorcycle cover over it, and nobody will bother it, especially if you put a 1 percent logo on it. When I got out of prison, I usually had a motorcycle waiting for me at a buddy's house.

They took me to the county jail just a few blocks away and booked me. There, I was together with three thousand or so other men in white who, for some reason, were allowed to forego a free night at the La Quinta for a free night at the downtown county jail.

County jail

County jail is where the desperate cases are.

Just imagine, one minute you're enjoying your latte, driving your Lexus, and listening to NPR while driving around the well-maintained Houston highways. You're in your pretty suit and colorful tie, with your pink gold Christophe Claret watch, talking to your wife on your Bluetooth. And the next minute, you're in the county jail.

You are suddenly thrown into a world you have never imagined you'd have to deal with. It is *totally* foreign to you—like going to Albania. You have no idea how you got where you are, and you don't speak the language needed to survive.

Everything is stripped away from you and put in a plastic bag inside a labeled box, waiting for you in case you survive. You are issued a loose-fitting white outfit—a shirt that's clean but ripped and ragged and pants that are loose and baggy but no belt. So the pants keep slipping off of you. You end up looking like some of the men you see walking downtown with their paints halfway down their buttocks and their underwear showing.

You have no watch, no cell phone, no car, no shoes but flip flops. There's no radio, but a TV's blaring in the corner. You have no family to comfort you, no friends to call and share this with. You are *alone*! You're alone in a group of thirty to forty-five other inmates who seem very comfortable with their surroundings, and for the most part, they are ignoring you, for which you are truly thankful. You do pray a lot more than you have ever done. At least God listens; you had seen that on KSBJ billboards around the beltway, usually shrugging it off. It seems like a good option now, the only one perhaps.

Some of your "roommates" look like they are high on drugs still. Some of them look beat up from the fight that got them there. Most of them have colorless tattoos, and all of them are looking at you funny, because your haircut and demeanor lets them know you don't belong there.

You feel trapped like an animal in a cage. Not that you are an animal, but you are convinced some of them around you are.

The first days are horrible. You cannot get used to the smell, the constant noise, the milling around, the division into racial groups, the lack of education, and the absence of a decent vocabulary. You hear the F word from almost all sides. There is a phone on the wall without a dial pad, but you have no idea how it functions. You feel like Daniel in the lion's den and are praying God will send an angel to prevent them from having you for lunch.

Most jails are overcrowded. The jailers are often overworked and sometimes overwhelmed. They have no idea what explosive characters they shoved in cages together. Some of the guys in the county jail, or "in county," are volatile with short fuses.

Some have never been locked up and are worried sick. For most of them, this is not their first rodeo, and they consider county to be easy time. They know the ropes, speak the language, have learned survival mode, and are ready for violence if they have to.

Some of them are here for a payoff-for the gang. They made a hit, and are doing the time for it, but the gang knows and will take care of them inside and outside the prison system. One man did a job for the gang. He did ten years, and when he got out, he built a beautiful house on a four-acre lot with a brick fence all around it and brick Roman gables out front. He did the crime, did the time, and then got his paycheck from the boss. The gang's leaders were pleased, and I guess he was too. I could take you to his house today; he still lives there.

County jail the first time is very scary—a fast learn-or-die experience. From there, you are transferred to prison, which is a survival-of-the-fittest scenario in some cases. The second time you get arrested, and every time after that, the county jail is more like a playground of bullies. You can get used to everything, even insanity.

Trial

While you're in county, if you cannot afford a lawyer, you will be appointed one. What they don't tell you is that the one they appoint to you is usually not too happy to *have* to deal with you. I have heard this story from so many inmates. The court-appointed attorney is just ready to get this over with and usually tries to talk you into pleading guilty and/or plea bargaining, so he or she can get on with his life.

The attorney will meet with you a few times while you're in the county jail and listen to your sob story (or your case, if he's a good one). Then he will say something like this: "If you plead guilty, you will only get fifteen years, but if you don't, and your case goes to trial, you might get twenty-five or thirty years. You know what a conservative bunch there is in this county and how all they want to do is lock you up and throw away the key. They are just a group of angry oilfield rednecks ready to put you where the sun doesn't shine. But if you plead guilty, you won't have to face them. And after you do your time, you can still get out and have a normal live."

He basically scares you to death. And you don't know what's true or not. You're on the inside, and he is smart; he wears a suit, he studied law, and he is assigned to help you. But is he helping you? Much of that cheap help ended up being very cheap indeed—or costly if you count the years taken away from men by the smart guy with the suitcase and the manila folders.

In all my time in prison, I have talked to many, many men who went through this scenario exactly—and who are *so* sorry that they did this. Some of them were *not* guilty but were terrified by their attorney, who just wanted a quick buck and to get this over with. He did not have the inmate's best interest in mind but, rather, his own.

One attorney told the inmate he was assigned to, "If you have sex with me, I will get you off easy, but if you don't I'll have you put away." That inmate is serving twenty-five years now for standing up for what his conscience told him was right.

What the court-appointed attorney does *not* tell you is this: He wants your case to be over with so he can get you out of his life and take a million-dollar lawsuit case where he can charge 30 percent and pay for his expensive toys. You are doing away with fifteen of the best years of your live. The jury might actually be favorable to you and give you only five or even two years. The living conditions in prisons are sometimes inhumane. There is a great chance of you being abused. You might have to fight and hurt somebody for your own survival. You will be poor; a pen and paper will be a prized possession. If any other inmate influences you to commit crimes *in* prison, you might get more time added.

You will have *no* physical contact with your wife and children.

Most likely, your parents will die while you're in prison, and you will not be able to attend the funeral. The world will slip by you. When you get out, you will no longer know how to use a smartphone, browse the internet, start a microwave, make decisions, trust people, find a good job, date, drive a car, and on and on. You won't be able to own a gun or vote.

You won't recognize sounds. One guy told me, when he got out, he heard a strange noise. He opened the windows, and the strange sound he didn't recognize was the wind in the leaves of the trees! He had not heard that in many years, because they keep the trees cut away in a circle around prison compounds to prevent escape.

You won't remember how to relate to people. One inmate told me that, in twenty years, he did not get *one* visit or *one* piece of mail. The isolation can be horrible.

Laugh or cry! There is not much laughter in prison, and you better cry under your blankets when you do, or you will be ridiculed.

So here you are, in front of a judge. (Now remember, previously I broke in to a dead judge's house, and I found a safe full of cocaine). I was worried that the law wasn't exactly on my side. Because of my "expert" advice from my attorney, I plead guilty. The hammer came down, the judgment was called, and I was carted off.

Next case

The courts are usually booked up, a few hundred cases and a year behind, so the mill must grind. Humanity is lost in legal lingo and business of the courts.

Back in the county jail, you get used to the daily routine. Breakfast was at 3:00 a.m., but I always slept through it. Why did the feeding times commence so early? Well, if you have to feed three thousand people in a lunchroom that holds only two hundred, you have to start early, or lunch will run into breakfast. You sit down to eat, and after five minutes, an officer will tell you to get up and leave. You'd better wolf it down quickly or throw it in the trash.

Lunch was at 10:00 a.m., usually the best meal, served on hard plastic trays with five compartments. The five compartments were filled with carbohydrates—potatoes, macaroni, bread, cupcake—and a small piece of overcooked chicken. For a while in the Texas Prison System they served TVP (textured vegetable protein)—meat made out of soya beans. But it was *so* horrible tasting, everybody called it dog food, few actually ate it, and even fewer enjoyed it. It took a riot in one of the prisons to bring that to a stop—no more TVP.

Most county jails have several buildings, or several wings. Most buildings are divided into three Pods. You end up in 4 Building, A Pod and so on,

This is going to be your new home for an undetermined amount of time. There are bunk beds. Often the pod divides itself by race; we are much more at ease with that, even though we don't talk about it much. You sleep on the bottom bunk and hope the guy in the upper bunk doesn't drool. If it' very overcrowded, which I have seen often, there are "mattresses" (three-inch thick foam) on the floor between the bunk beds. That means, if you have to use the bathroom at night, it's possible you step on somebody's body somewhere and get whacked for doing that.

County is a river of humans—always somebody coming in or going out. They get arrested, they come in, they're released a few days later, and they go home. They've been classified and are going to the Big House; they leave. If they get in a fight with another inmate on Pod A, one of them might end up on Pod B, and the other, on Pod C. The prison system does a lot to prevent violence against other inmates.

After a week or several months of total boredom in the county jail, where you play a lot of checkers and chess, you get put on a white bus to the Big House, to the classification unit. From there, you get a bus ticket to the Big House—Galveston for me usually.

CHAPTER 17

SURVIVING IN PRISON

The classification unit

One of the oldest and most centrally located units in Texas is where you are processed *in* and *out* of the prison system—the classification unit in Huntsville. The Texas Department of Justice (TDCJ) deemed it efficient to use this unit as an entry and exit point. When you arrive there, you're put in a cell by yourself. Since your jailers do not know much about you—you haven't been evaluated yet—they're not sure if they can trust you to kill somebody or if you're too much of a wimp and will become somebody's toy. That's why almost all cells there have only *one* occupant. This gives you time to think and time to adjust to your new future, your life inside TDCJ.

There is an old poem I read years ago that keeps coming back to me over the years. Especially every time I got locked up. It's called, "Department of Correction." These are a few of the lines I remember:

Department of Correction,
where all your faults are pointed out and stripped away
Department of Reflection,
where in the mirror you will see another man.
Department of Rejection,
where no one cares who you were or who you are
Department of Dissection,
where your whole life is split apart and laid all bare.

It was a poem that had intrigued me for many years; I never realized how real it would become to me. The department of corrections previously was called "penitentiary"—an old English word that has as its roots in the word "penance." This word is still noticeable when the inmate calls his buddies and tells them he is in the "pen." With penance, of course, there is a goal behind locking up a violator of the law—the hope is that if you punish violators, they will perform the act of penance or "repentance." Give them time to think about their mischievous acts, and perhaps they will "repent," come to their senses, and realize their previous actions were a big mistake. And, thus, it will not happen again.

The first morning at the classification unit, you are "welcomed," into the penal system and classified. You spend most of the day standing in front of a lot of different desks, where many questions are being asked. At some stations, your jailers take things from you; at some stations they give you things. At some stations, they ask you a lot of questions. At some stations, they give you a lot of instructions.

The first desk is where they take your name away; you get fingerprinted and issued a TDCJ number. Mine was 711332. From that point on, your name is no longer important. I felt like I lost "*me*" that day.

The next station is where you stood behind a low screen and are instructed to take *all* your clothes off. Your clothes and all your other possessions—watch, belt, shoes, and so on—are carefully placed in a white and blue file box with your TDCJ number on it. That will be the last you see of them until your release. You're given a pair of white baggy underwear, which is the only thing you'll wear the rest of the day.

Many more stations follow. One of them is a doctor, who gives you a quick physical and cavity search. After he weighs you, he inoculates you against the more prevalent diseases; your arm will be sore for a while—just like somebody punched you.

At one desk, a psychiatrist looks at your paperwork and asks you a bunch of questions about your past jobs and interests. I never realized how significant that short interview was in placement or classification, which determines which prison you go to and what job you get to do while you do "time."

The whole day, there are a hundred men in front of you and a hundred behind you, all in the baggy white outfits, some worn to rags, some crisp and clean. Then you go back into a holding tank, a cell that has twenty-five bunk beds and fifty men. You spend one more night there in the middle of total strangers.

The next day brings more of the same. This time, it's not so much necessities like shoes and clothing but a thorough evaluation.

Just an honest observation—I was arrested many times, and I went through this process many times. Not *one* time did I feel like any of the TDCJ employees treated me with anything but dignity and respect. I was roughhoused by policemen, rightfully so at times. I have been beat up by other inmates.

Neither during these evaluations, nor during any time I served was I treated with disdain by prison guards, or officers as they prefer to be called.

Not one TDCJ prison employee ever did me harm.

Maybe you have heard horror stories of prisoner mistreatment at the hands of officers. I spent twenty years in prison and have grown to respect the men in gray. I think the system figured out that, if they treat an inmate with respect, he is not likely to assault an officer. And they must have adjusted their training program accordingly. The danger in any prison for me was never the gray suits but, rather, the other inmates. After running for several years, it was actually good to get a break and be treated fairly normal.

One desk you stand in front of has several people who interview you on your alleged gang activity. If you were in a gang and denied it, usually your tattoos gave you away; also they had your files. If you'd spent time in prison before, all your behavior was distinctly spelled out. You could lie, but if you had a case that was gang related, they would read it out to you.

They have your arrest records, what the police report says, and so on. My police report was not very long, as I wouldn't talk when I was arrested. I took the "you have the right to remain silent" literally. It made the cops very upset. I gave them my driver's license but would not say anything. I found out through life that people's mouths *always* give them away. If you spend enough time with somebody, the person usually will spill his or her whole life history to you. And when the police arrest a person who does not talk, it just drives them bezonkers. Perhaps they haven't had time to study the Miranda rights that they so quickly quote. But if you don't tell them anything, they do not know you robbed a store or sold drugs or anything—not without proof. Silence is golden—if you can put up with a little harassment from frustrated policemen.

At the end of the day, you've either spilled your guts or had them spilled on the table in front of you by people in suits wearing badges. You're put back in the tank, or in solitary, for one more night. The next day, you *catch the chain*.

Catching the chain is prison slang for going by bus somewhere. But before they put you on the bus, they usually put handcuffs on you; if you have an aggravated sentence, you might get ankle chains also. The handcuffs on your stomach and the chains from your ankles connect somewhere around your belt, and severely prohibit movement. That's the idea, right?

Life in prison

Your transport *to* the prison is usually in a bus, not a Greyhound but, rather, a white school bus without any conveniences. Steel seats, gray cushions. In the middle of the bus, there are two stainless steel toilets, no walls. So if you have to take a dump, you sit where the back half of the bus is staring at you, and where the whole bus can smell you. It is not a whole lot of fun if you have to go and have to wipe your behind while you're handcuffed to somebody else. Don't try that at home.

Prison is not easy. It is *not* fun. It is *not* air-conditioned, unless you're in the hospital or unless you're a minor. As a minor, you'll be put in an educational facility, sort of a military-style reform school. If you catch the chain and have to go to the hospital in Galveston, you have to endure a very uncomfortable bus ride first. Nothing about prison is fun; you don't hear a lot of laughing there.

Your new home away from home is actually far, far away from home. Most prisons are built away from cities and towns, usually on the outskirts of small towns nobody has heard of. Generally, there's a two-or three-mile-long dead-end road in between open pastures or swamps. That way, if you feel like escaping, you have to clear a few miles of grasslands, which gives the K9 police dogs plenty of time to pick up your scent and catch up with you. Some can even follow your scent when you get in a car; one of them even walked himself to exhaustion but did catch the escapee.

When you first arrive in prison, you're again put in a sort of holding tank. There are basically three different housing situations.

In solitary, you are alone in a cell for twenty-three hours and only allowed one hour to shower or go to the recreation area, or rec.

Bunk bed cells open up a few times a day for you to go in and out. All are connected to a day room, where you can socialize with about three dozen men who sleep in their cells at night.

Dormitories are similar to cubicles, twice the size of a bed. There are no internal walls except the low ones around the beds. You can walk around the dorms that house around a hundred men each. The dormitories give you the most "freedom."

When you arrive at the prison, you will usually be put in a cell first with a cellie. If you behave well and don't get any cases, then you might be moved to the dorms. If you are in a bad dorm, there might be a lot of racial tension and fights or other eruptions of violence, sometimes over the fact that the wrong TV station has been selected by a certain person.

The first thing I did when I was locked up usually was write my wife. I'd let her know where I was and ask her to come see me ASAP and put some money on my books.

One time when I got arrested, I asked the judge if I could have some time to get my stuff in order. He allowed me two weeks to do that before I was to report at the prison.

I asked my dad if I could store my guns at his house. He said OK. Well, my dad was up in age at that time. I arrived at his house with my pickup truck loaded with guns. He usually got up slowly and did his regular morning routine. He would take a shower, shave, and comb his hair; put in his false teeth, find batteries for his hearing aids, and clean his glasses; make himself some coffee; and then go to the living room to watch the Fox News morning show. He used to joke that, in the morning, he had to put his whole his body back together. When he went to bed, he laid his whole body on his nightstand—his eyes (glasses), his teeth (dentures), and his ears (hearing aid).

While he was doing his morning routine, I unloaded my truck. First, I unloaded the guns and stacked them against the wall near the front door. Then I continued all around the living room standing guns and rifles against the walls. When there was no more room, I put them straight up against the furniture, all around the coffee table, and leaned them against the chairs and the couch.

Then I got my pistols. I laid them out on the coffee table, on the chairs, on the couch, on the armrests, and on the back of the couch. I did this until there was no more room to walk or sit in the living room. I had quite a collection of firearms; they are a good investment, always worth more with age when properly handled.

I had some large knives and other self-defense instruments. Among them was a stun gun that would release two sharp, piercing arrows connected to steel wires to the gun. When you make good contact, it will knock out a cow. I laid all the rest of the stuff on the free space between the pistols.

It took me almost exactly the same time as my dad took for his morning routine. So by the time he walked in to the living room, I was done, and there was no room for him to sit or stand anywhere.

He stood in the door of the living room and patiently observed how I'd turned his living room into an armory. He took a deep breath and said, "I hope the local sheriff is not about to come visit you right now."

He had several hope chests. We wrapped the guns in sheets and laid them in the hope chests. The pistols we put inside socks on top of the guns. We packed his chests full. He had a toolbox that came from the back of a truck sitting in his garage. We filled it up also. Some of the guns that he liked he put in his gun cabinet. It was large and had two large windows that were rounded out toward you. This allowed a round plate to be loaded with guns and turned similarly to the gun displays at dealers.

I went to prison for quite a few years that time. My dad would visit me about once a month if the unit I was in wasn't far away. Then, when I needed some money, he would pawn one of the guns. I had it pretty comfortable that hitch and never ran out of money; the guns were a worthy investment. When I was released from prison, all the guns were gone, but I still had the gold stash in Galveston (map in the back of the book).

The first week in prison, I was evaluated, not by the institution but by the inmates. This is the normal process I later found out. They sent a scout to the cell to check me out—determining my age, size, ability, and so on. Then a few days later, they send a guy to your cell to beat you up—not a giant killer, but somebody about your size and age. They put a scout at your door, the fighter is let in, and he starts beating you up. "Welcome to the prison system." You either let him beat you up and you will be treated like a sissy the rest of your time, or you stand your ground.

I always stood my ground, using a few basic ground rules.

Rule number 1, anything goes. Rule number 2, anything can be used as a weapon. I had learned some judo and jujitsu when I was on the outside. I did some wrestling in high school and used every trick of the trade to prevent my untimely demise or damage to extremities.

Somewhere during the fight, I threw baby powder in his eyes, which gave me a slight advantage. Using some judo technique, I threw him against the bars of the cell. This did some serious bruising to his ribs.

Suddenly, the lookout said, "*Stop*." An officer was making his rounds; we stopped fighting, I stood against my bunk reading a book and acting nonchalant. As soon as the officer stepped away from the pod, we were given the go-ahead, and it was on again.

The guy started pounding me. I was not a very good boxer. I took a few hits and then grabbed his fist and drew him past me. I lowered my head and pulled his nose against the top of my head. This broke his nose, and the fight was over. He left. Afterward, I was treated with some respect.

Later, I was to meet the lieutenant of the gang. He asked me to join. I declined. No matter what gangs there were in the prisons I was in, I never joined. You had the option. If you joined, you paid dearly to get in and paid dearly to get out, sometimes with your life. If you did not want to join, they did not force you. But they also wouldn't protect you or give you the other "fringe" benefits of membership.

I'd never been in a gang on the outside of the prison, and I made up my mind never to join a gang inside the prison. I never did. One time on the street, a guy called me a "b – – ch" several times, and I got fed up with him and hit him one time. I must have hit the right spot. He fell down and hit his head on the concrete, which knocked him out. But since he was in a gang, as punishment, the gang gave me two minutes against the wall. That was where two of the biggest guys get to use you as a punching bag while you stand silently against the wall. It hurts, but you'd better not move or fight back, or the next level might be un-survivable.

When my girlfriend saw my naked torso three days later, she started crying; it still looked badly bruised. This let me know the gang never is and will never be your best friend. Gangs are really a bunch of bullies who find strength in numbers. With just their gang insignia—a tattoo, a handkerchief, or a vest—they let people know that others will come help them out when they need it. But on their own, they're just as scared as a lost alley cat.

While I stayed on the dorms, one of the larger men, "Boss," tormented one of the smaller new guys, called Albert. Albert had a plan to stop this. He would take a shower and keep a piece of soap; over time, this piece of soap had grown to the size of a baseball. After a few weeks of mistreatment by the bully, Albert waited until the big guy was asleep.

He put the soap ball in a sock and crawled over to Boss's cubicle. Swinging the sock in a circle and winding it up in speed, he let it land in the middle of Boss's mouth. It not only took out most of his teeth but also busted his lips and his tongue. By the time the officers showed up, Albert was seemingly sound asleep, awoken by the commotion. The ball of soap was slowly melting in one of the toilets. No fingerprints; they never figured out who did it. But Boss knew.

I saw it all happen; I was lying there awake a few cubicles over. In prison and out, it is better not to get involved in a dogfight; you will get bit too. Boss never looked the same again; it took him a few years to have partials made. He lost a lot of weight, probably because he couldn't eat right anymore. Two good things that came out of that was that he never bullied anybody again, and he treated Albert with a little more respect after that.

Chow line could be a violent situation, not only because of what inmates could possibly put in your food, but this was also where different gangs and groups were in a position to act out orders or grievances. One man told me he would not scoop the food where the spoon was. He would take the spoon out, tap the spoon empty, and take a scoop from the other side of the bowl. I asked him why he did that; he said somebody once crushed a glass bottle and ground it really small, made sure he was in the chow line in front of the man he wanted to harm, deposited the glass in the food, and positioned the spoon right there.

When the next guy scooped up the food, he had no idea he'd just loaded his tray with glass-embedded food. When he started eating, not only did the glass cut his tongue, he also swallowed some, causing internal damage as well. I told you this chapter would have some violence in it.

One man whore fused to join a gang had been targeted by one of the enforcers of a gang. This enforcer was six foot five and three hundred pounds. Normally, he would not have had a chance, but when they were outside in the rec yard, the little guy jumped on the back of the three hundred-pound dude. First he removed the lower partial out of his mouth and held it to the big guy's throat. He told him he would cut his jugular vein if he tried anything else, which would have been true. Then he jumped off. The big guy and him actually became friends after that—mutual respect based on violence, but still respect.

What happened next made me a very rich man one day, but I did not clip the coupons till a little while later.

I was in the chow line. The food servers were on our left, and to our right was an iron railing, which was there to keep us going forward and prevent anybody else from the chow hall jumping in line. In front of me was a black guy. He was an El Camino member. I didn't know his name. In front of him was a Mexican guy. His name was Alberto, and he was a lieutenant in the gang. As we were inching forward, I saw the black guy pull out a shank. Actually he had it taped to the palm of his right hand. This way, if he got in a fight, his opponent(s) could not knock the knife out of his hand.

He raised his hand with the blade and was fixing to stab Alberto. Even though what I was about to do would put me in administrative segregation (ad seg), I felt like saving a life was more important than that.

I acted quickly. Right when his right arm was outstretched the highest, fixing to come down and stab Alberto, I grabbed his right arm just above the elbow and swung it in an arch to the right and down. I'd made that half circle so forceful that, when his arm hit the iron railing, it broke his bones in two places all the way through. He fell on the ground, wincing in pain, knife still taped to his hand.

He couldn't move, disabled by the pain. I was glad it didn't cause a riot. Some people think I have Spanish roots, but I don't. I didn't want the inmates to know it was a gang fight.

There is usually at least one officer in the chow hall. He was there in a few seconds and got on his radio to report a fight and get assistance.

At that point, the unit went on lock down and all necessary officers came to the fight scene. All the officers present saw the knife still taped to the El Camino guy's hand, and the guilty verdict was easily passed. I was taken in for an interview but did *not* get a case or restrictions at all. They were actually pleasantly surprised that I had prevented a murder on their unit. It's not a pleasant task to notify the next of kin, usually a mother, that her beloved boy had been stabbed in the chow line by a coward from behind.

What I didn't find out till later that day was that the Mexican guy, Alberto, was a lieutenant in the Mexican gang. He was high up in rank in the gang, and I just saved his life from an El Camino member; it was an ordered hit. Alberto's bodyguard count went up after that.

Later, when I was out, a gang general gave me permission to rob a judge's house that was loaded. They had the house infiltrated with a Mexican maid and a Mexican yard man. They basically knew all about the judge and the house. When the judge died, they "gave" me the house. I robbed the house and was $3 million. The GPS locations of the gold bars and gold coins I uncovered there are in the back of the book. But that's another chapter.

Prison is a lonely place. There is little laughter, and there is no crying, except under the blankets or in the shower. It is a hard place to live, like I said before, not because of the officers but because of the other inmates. If they only understood that life doesn't have to be miserable if they didn't make it so hard on everybody else. But stupid people do stupid things, and desperate people do desperate things.

I've served several sentences, from one year to ten years. All that time, they make you believe the normal world is in the prison. But when you get out, you find out how abnormal it really is. You make *no* decisions in prison. You're told when to eat, what to eat, when to go to sleep and where, where to walk, when to walk, and how to dress. When you get out, you don't know how to make decisions anymore. When people who spend much time in solitary confinement get out, they just want to stay in their room.

There is one exception. The faith-based pods initiated in the TDCJ have created a totally different environment than any prison or jail I've experienced. But more about that later.

In prison, not a whole lot of people care about you, and subsequently no one asks you many questions. When I got out one time and went to a church, this guy who helped me asked me a lot of questions—how I was, where I'd been, if I was OK, and so on. I wasn't used to that. He actually cared. But it made me nervous, and I pushed him away; I shouldn't have. He loved me and let me know by showing interest—showing he cared. But I didn't know how to be loved and accepted. I blamed the church for giving me the cold shoulder and left, even though I had given them the cold shoulder. I expected them to serve me up their love and religion on a sectioned-off prison tray at 3:00 a.m., 10:00 p.m. and 5:00 p.m. Life on the outside takes a lot of adjusting if you've been confined any length of time.

Life in a federal penitentiary is vastly different from life in a state prison. At the time I was there, you were not allowed to smoke in the Texas State Prison System, but it was condoned in the federal pen. For smokers, that was a big relief; if you depend on nicotine to keep you from beating me up, please smoke one.

Federal prisons appear to have more money in their budget. The buildings are nicer, the beds are thicker, the doors seem more impenetrable, and the uniforms of the officers are khaki and tan instead of blue and gray.

I made a friend in the Federal Prison about ninety miles northeast of Houston. His name was Brice. Brice had taken female hormones and had long blond hair. When you first saw him, you suspected somebody smuggled a beautiful blond into the prison. One evening when we were talking privately, Brice told me that, all his life, the devil told him he was a woman, but he really wanted to be a man. Brice was a troubled soul. On the outside, he looked like a woman; on the inside he felt like a man. And the further he advanced with his transformation, the worse he felt. He told me several times he wished he could undo what he'd done so far. His family was wealthy and supported him financially, allowing him to buy any hormone or have any surgery he wanted. But Brice just wanted to be how he was born to be. I spent much time with him.

The chow hall at the federal pen looks like a McDonalds. There are coffee machines, milk dispensers, skillets for you to cook your own spread, microwaves, toasters—all you can eat and drink. We often called it club fed.

There was a guy in there who robbed a business on this side of the Texas border, shot a man, and wounded him a little. Then he drove across the state line into Louisiana, so his crime became a two-state federal crime. They locked him up in federal prison. You know why he did that? He could no longer afford his heart medicine, and he figured, if he was locked up in a federal prison, they would hand it to him for free at the pill window.

CHAPTER 18

THE GREAT ESCAPE MISTAKE

Out of all the things in my criminal career, this was the biggest mistake I made. I escaped from a prison. In retrospect, that was a *big* mistake. I would never do it again, and I would never advise anybody to do it. They automatically tack five to ten years to your sentence because you "broke the law" by not submitting to your punishment. And escape is a felony, an embarrassment to the prison system.

So, please understand, this was wrong. I should have never done it. But I was young and full of energy and youthful ignorance. I paid for it dearly. *After* an escape and when you get caught, which you eventually will, if you get locked up again, you will be considered "an escape risk"—rightfully so. And you usually spend *years* in solitary confinement with magnetic stickers over your door warning every officer to be very careful in handling you, as you might escape again.

As I believe I've given you enough to let you know this was a bad idea, here' how I escaped.

To mount a successful escape, you need a few things:

1.) Time

2.) Tools

3.) Thoughts

You need to plan your escape carefully. You need to know all about the *time* of the officers—when they work, how they work, when they come to work, when they leave for home, what shift, and what vehicle they drive.

You need to *think* out your escape. You need to know first *how* to get out from behind the steel doors, concrete walls, and barbed wire. But you also need to know what you're going to do when you get on the other side of the wall. That is the most important thing, really. Otherwise, the hounds will track you down. Or you might get shot attempting to escape, while you land on the razor wire. I have seen that happen.

My favorite books to read are escape books—like *Escape from Colditz* and *Shantaram*. It always puzzled me why there werel, 500 men in a prison and only 1 escaped! What was different about this guy? Was he smarter? Does he think more? Those guys had always been my secret heroes.

Escape from Colditz is a book about all the men who escaped from the clutches of the German Army during World War II. The Germans planned to put them in the most secure prison they had. It was in a V of two rivers, on a rock. You couldn't tunnel through, they thought. You couldn't swim across, they thought. The book describes the brilliant minds of American, British, Dutch, Polish, and many other prisoners of war who plotted together and during all their time in Colditz during the end of World War II. They made 175 escape attempts, many successfully. They made uniforms and passports and even money. I highly recommend the book as an example of courage under extremely negative circumstances.

Shantaram is another one, though it isn't so much about the escape from an Australian prison, instead exploring, What is an Australian escaped prisoner to do? He ended up going to India, living in shantytowns, and helping where he could. He even made a daring raid into Afghanistan with the mujahedeen—the guerrilla-type military outfits led by the Muslim Afghan warriors fighting the Russian occupation.

But I was not in Afghanistan or Germany. I was really at war with myself. During that time, though, I saw myself as being at war with the system.

Time

I studied many of the guards, called officers, and observed their work schedule. Most of them worked twelve hour days, four days in a row—from 6:00 a.m. till 6:00 p.m., with a short window of shift change. They would work four days on and five days off, and sometimes, they worked overtime; sometimes, they swapped shifts with a coworker.

My final target was an older man. He was a contractor. His shift was eight to five. He drove a white Ford F-150. He was a little over sixty, bald headed, about five foot six, and heavyset. A very kind man. I had worked in the furniture factory with him, where he was responsible for the heavy-duty planing machines. We ran large sheets through there to make tabletops and desk tops that ended up in federal buildings; probably the same judge that had put us there was sitting behind a desk made by us inmates.

This particular guard's habits were always the same—easy to follow, easy to study, easy to remember. I didn't write anything down. If I did, it was in Spanish. He parked in the same parking spot every day, locked his vehicle, came in through the same gate, and stayed in the unit for lunch. He always ate at the ODR (officer's dining room) and walked out the gate at 5:05 p.m. carrying his large green thermos bottle.

He, or more his vehicle, would become my means of putting a great distance between me and the prison. My goal was Houston. I had to get back home to my gold stash in Galveston, rent another apartment, buy a few cars, and get back to work. From where I was, Highway 59 South or Interstate 45 were the quickest routes to home base.

Tools

Since the local hardware store was sort of off limits for us, I would steal. I stole *anything* I saw lying around, lying on the ground, or left on a desk. I stole from anybody—clerks, chaplains, officers, contractors, anybody who left anything; once they turned their backs, it was gone. I needed clothes. The white and bright orange outfits made you stand out quite a bit should you be walking on the side of the road near a prison. So I made some of it.

The pants were easy. We were issued pants, usually only one pair. But if you bribed the guy in necessities, he would give you an extra pair. So I had two. The pair that would become my escape pants, I left soaking in coffee for weeks. Even instant coffee has an excellent side effect of keeping you in not just caffeine but also brown coloring. I checked the pants now and then. First, they were skin color. When I kept soaking them, eventually they turned a nice chocolate brown. Then I bartered for some starch and laid them on my iron bed soaked in starch. They almost looked like a nice pair of pants from a suit.

I did a similar thing with my shirt. We were served beets, red beets; and as much as I liked to eat them, I took them home in my cup and asked anybody near me in the dining room to swap me the beets for my meat and my bread and so on. They are probably the best natural source of red dye known to men. I soaked the shirt in the crushed red beets, and in a few days, I had the prettiest red shirt you'd ever seen on a prison yard. I just couldn't wear it. I hid it with the pants in a stash in my cell. During several shakedowns, it was never found.

Next up was the jacket. That was a necessity, as I'd planned my escape during the winter. Most prisons are surrounded by a large cleared area of grass and, sometimes, swamp. I didn't want to get eaten by mosquitoes or step on a snake. Winter would be the best time to be fully dressed. The clothing would not only help me escape the cold but also serve as a cover or hideaway.

We had volunteers come into the prison, and some of them were new, naive. During the summer, one of them had taken his jacket off and laid it on a table. While nobody was watching, I snatched the jacket, went to the shower, put it on under my white prison shirt, and went immediately to my pod. Some of the officers strip-searched you going back to your dorm. Some didn't. I knew this one officer alone by a gate would just let me walk by, and he did. This jacket became my prized possession. Perhaps, it would be my ticket to the outside in relative obscurity or, when I was outside, my prevention from detection. I really needed it to walk from the prison fence to the pickup truck without attracting attention from the guy with the shotgun in the tower.

As for shoes, we were able to buy New Balance sneakers brown, black, and white, but also ankle-high leather boots. I knew that, during an escape, you wanted to keep your feet dry. Wet feet and your whole body would get miserable. Also you do *not* want to break or sprain your ankle. Most survivalists advise you never to run in an unfamiliar territory. When you break your ankle, your escape is over. Therefore, I'd bought the ankle-high leather boots. They might have been hot in the summer, but they were very strong and dependable. My wardrobe was complete.

Thoughts

I studied the unit—the high barbed wire fences, the guard towers, the lights and the razor wire—looking for a hole, a weakness somewhere. I did a lot of jogging, partly for staying in shape and partly to scout the perimeter. If your life is spent running from the law, you'd better be in good shape. The officers were used to me jogging around the walking track right inside the fence, getting out of breath, and doubling over to catch my breath or even leaning close to the fence to see the construction. It was mostly well made, galvanized four-inch posts, twelve feet high, and securely attached with heavy-duty clamps. Razor wire stretched over the whole perimeter.

Except in one spot. I got so excited when I found the spot where there was a hole, a clear hole. It was near the gate. There is, in every prison, a very large, wide gate where vehicles like busses come through to drop off and pick up inmates. That gate slides down a track pushed and pulled by electrical motors. Where the gate slid open and closed, the razor wire would have gotten hopelessly caught, so they left it off; that way, the gate could slide open easily.

Also at dark, the light poles were positioned all around the perimeter, every fifty feet. High-intensity sodium lights cast a bright orange glow. I studied them also—where they were, when they came on, when they went off, what direction the light was thrown, and what shadows they left. Did they overlap or not? Were some not functioning, flickering at times? I would run until it got dark; with the daylight saving changes, sometimes, they left us out until it was dark. We had to be in at a certain time, but that time gave me an hour of observation of the unit in the dark. And lo and behold, there was an unlit spot, in the crevice of a building. And on top of that, it was fairly close to the gate where I'd observed the hole in the razor wire.

The fact those two items, the hole in the fence and the unlit spot in the corner of a building close to that hole, were in such proximity solidified the plan to use that as my exit spot. I know it was a bad idea. Don't try this at home.

Also, believe it or not, my favorite balding contractor parked his Ford F-150 pretty close to that same gate. It seemed like the pieces were coming together. I didn't need a key for the vehicle. I could bust the window with my elbow and start the truck by jamming a flat screwdriver in the ignition. I'd tried it many times, and it always worked.

I was ready to go. I hadn't told anybody; you cannot trust anyone in the prison. They will snitch on you for no reason at all or perhaps hoping to get some time taken off their sentence. I'd seen groups escape, and usually, one was too slow and couldn't keep up and drug everybody down.

The only ones who made it as a group were the Texas Seven. Their big mistake was staying together. They attracted the attention of the campground owner where they were staying, and he called the law. All of them but one, who committed suicide, were caught shortly after that. If they would have spread out and traveled alone, it would have been a lot harder to catch them. But they felt invincible one of them told me. They are now on death row because they killed a security guard at an Oshman's Sporting Goods store, showering his car with bullets. So I went alone.

Now or Never

I waited till the winter. It was getting dark by five, totally dark by six. As soon as it was dark, I waited in the spot along the wall where the light didn't shine. I could see the officer on the nearest tower walking around. He had his back toward me and was making a circle on his little balcony.

I sprinted for the fence, heart pounding. Nobody saw me. He came back around, made another circle. When he had his right shoulder toward me, I started climbing. Sure enough, when I came to the top of the fence, there was no razor wire. I slung my leg over and climbed down. I stood still at the bottom.

It is amazing how blind even a guard on a tower eventually becomes; they never see anything, so they don't expect to ever see anything. He came back around. I was wearing a red shirt, the brown pants and the jacket I'd stolen from the volunteer six months ago. The officer in the tower must have thought I was the contractor. I walked to the Ford F-150 and tried the door first; it was unlocked. It was a serious breach of protocol for the contractor to leave his vehicle unlocked. I slammed the door, making the normal sound a working man would make. I jammed the screwdriver in to the ignition and drove away.

The last guard shack recognized my truck; it was getting dark. I waved the fake plastic badge I'd made and drove into freedom—*not* speeding. Another stupid mistake a lot of escapees made was getting pulled over for speeding. No I was a law-abiding "escapee" and kept looking in the mirror, but I never saw the glow of bright flashing red and blue lights. The little white Ford truck drove like a train. It was a very common vehicle; there are more white trucks on the road than any other color. I blended right in. By the time they found me missing, I was 120 miles away; it was a "home" run. I was happy with my freedom, but it came with a dear price tag later.

I made it to Highway 59. It was busy, like always. I blended into the traffic. After about an hour, I crossed Beltway 8; fifteen more minutes, and I crossed the 610 Loop. I went from Highway 59 to Interstate 45 South and drove to Galveston, where I kept my gold stash buried by the nine abandoned *Galveston Sentinel* houses. I used my "treasure map"; I'd buried these gold reserves in similar locations. It took me a few minutes of digging and probing in the dark, but I did finally find a roll of Krugerrands I'd buried there for "such a time as this." That gave me $40,000 to get started. I drove the truck to a residential neighborhood, stole a tarp from another vehicle, and covered the white Ford, like it was there preserved in long-term parking. Walked to a hotel, I acted like I'd just checked out of my room. I hailed a taxi and took it to downtown Houston. I rented a nice apartment, and I was back in business.

The next time I got caught, they added the escape to my charges. There were a bunch of very angry prison officers who had to work almost twenty-four hour per day to try to catch the one who got away. The warden was fired for failure to keep the public safe. I would never do it again, I promised myself in the many lonely nights in solitary confinement.

Here is my advice to those young ones locked up: If you get locked up, do your time.

CHAPTER 19

HOW ONE TOUCH CHANGED ME

Prison is a hard place. There is no laughter, no joy, no open hearts. There is *no* good touching.

When you are touched by another inmate, it is usually bad touching. It can be a fist or another form of unexpected violence, or worse, like sexual assault. There used to be a lot of sexual assaults in the prison system; this often resulted in suicide. There, officers in TDCJ have had a lot of training in inmate-to-inmate assault and suicides, and both have gone down a lot over the years.

Just imagine. You're suddenly locked away from your family, with no place to hide and no one to call. Not only are you feeling like a forgotten person, you're also subject to many habits and vices that are prevalent.

Some men felt like the only way to escape the abuse was to end their lives. Much education and training of staff has helped prevent this. The only way for the staff to protect the vulnerable ones was to put them in a cell by themselves. One of my best friends did time in prison like that; he was small and had a seventy-year sentence for robbing stores while he was on cocaine. He couldn't protect himself, so the system did it for him by locking him in a cell by himself.

I lived in prison for many years and did not experience that evil. But I also did not experience very much good touching.

Until I met this one man.

I enrolled in a mentor program; it was fairly new then in the Texas Prison System.

They would assign you a mentor.

Men from the outside came in, two Thursdays a month, at 6:00 p.m. They were the mentors; we were the mentees. I did exactly that, and it changed my life forever.

I hadn't been at this prison very long when somebody told me about the mentor program, and I signed up.

Thursday afternoon at around 5:00 p.m., I received my lay-in slip and was called to the front and told to report to the chapel. There was actually not a chapel built on that prison property yet, so they used several school rooms that were separated by movable hanging walls. The walls were removed, and it made a fairly large area to hold services in, about forty feet wide by fifty feet long, with two doors, one at the west side close to the window that looked out on the rec yard and one on the east side that looked toward the visitation area.

I didn't know what to expect really. I didn't even know what the word *mentor* stood for or what they would do for me. But I was selfish and greedy and was trying to get as much out of anybody that I could. Perhaps I'd get a pen or a notebook. Perhaps I could talk him into putting some money on my books or smuggling a letter out to my homeboys. I was always scheming to use and abuse the system. Joining the mentorship program was one of my ploys to better myself, often to the detriment of others. But it did not turn out that way.

I walked to the chapel; it was dusk and would be dark soon. There were about forty inmates lined up to go into the chapel. I knew there was no regular church service, as that was only on Sunday morning; the Catholic service was on Saturday evening. This was Thursday.

We waited in line close the chapel entrance on the right side of the yellow line. The officers and visitors were allowed to walk in the middle of the sidewalk. There were two yellow lines drawn on the sidewalk, one on each side about two feet from the grass. If you went one way, you walked on the right side of the yellow line. If you went the other way, you were on the other side of the sidewalk, also with a yellow line on your left side. This way, you would never run into another inmate head-on, where you could slip him contraband or a message or hit him in the face. We were kept separate from contact in many ways; this was one of them.

At about ten minutes till six, the picket door swung open, and a little more than a dozen free world men walked in. I had never seen any of them before. Most of them looked middle aged or retirement age.

We had to wait until they were in the chapel. Then we were allowed to go in. Some of the men were familiar with the system. When you walked in the door, there was a man with a checklist. He had all the names of the free world men listed on one side and the names of the prisoners who would be mentored by them on the other side.

The prisoners who *did* have a permanent mentor knew exactly where to go. After they had their names checked off by the mentor coordinator, a big smile appeared on their face. They walked straight toward their assigned mentor, and the two embraced in a big bear hug.

Here was proper touching. I had not seen that in a while.

Here were big smiles, on inmates who had little joy in their lives.

Here was outside contact. I was about to learn more about this.

I was stopped at the door by the mentor coordinator. He asked me if I had a mentor. I told him I did not. He said they had some extra free world men, and some did not have a mentee yet. So he wrote down my name on a list and walked me into the room.

He introduced me to a man called Jacob, who was sitting at a white plastic table in a steel chair. The table was eight feet long, but there were only four chairs by the table, two on each side. They did not want the men to sit too close together. I found out why later. Not only would it keep the noise down, so you could hear each other better, but it also allowed more privacy; the inmate could share more intimate details of his life with his mentor, without anybody else hearing it.

I sat down across from Jacob. He was middle aged, gray hair. I introduced myself; he told me his last name, which I instantly forgot because of what happened next.

I was forty years old, and I had never experienced this before.

We sat at the white plastic table across from each other, and Jacob reached both hands across the table from me and said, "Let's pray first."

I held his hands, my right with his left, and my left with his right.

Then Jacob started praying.

It wasn't loud or boisterous, just a simple heartfelt prayer.

The Nazarene Church I'd attended as a child had had a book of common prayer, and the priest would read one or two of those from the book each service. You could follow along, see each word as he prayed it. Not with Jacob. This was not a prepared prayer. It seemed like it came straight from his heart and mind. He was talking in a normal voice, as if he was speaking to a good friend.

Like I said earlier, I had not been touched properly normally for many years in the prison or outside. That was why, initially, just being touched with love shook me so much.

When his hands touched mine and he prayed that simple kind prayer over us, over me, over our meeting each other, whatever he said, it really did not matter.

It shook me to the core.

I had been a hardened criminal. I stole for a living. I broke into residences and businesses and took what I wanted. I had no conscience when it came to the consequences of my actions. I really did not care. I'd robbed the printshop, not only stealing the shop's inventory but going as far as imitating the owner's looks and going to *his* bank the next day dressed up like him and emptying his bank account. I did not care. I did not care that he now would not be able to pay his bills or feed his family and that perhaps he'd have to declare bankruptcy. It did not matter to me.

I had stolen cars, ran from the police, and worked with individuals much shadier than me; and I had done this for many years. Never once had I regretted my actions. Never once had I given it a second thought. Never once did I feel sorry or shame.

But suddenly, when Jacob touched me, a deep regret poured over me.

I felt sorry for what I had done, but I didn't know why.

He prayed, and I felt something I'd never felt before.

I felt like the world stood still. He probably prayed only about a hundred words, only one minute, perhaps two. But in those two minutes, I traveled back in time to when I first stole a crayon from the blackboard in school and ran around the corner so the teacher couldn't see me.

I saw myself stealing a bicycle from the rack in school and riding it home, throwing it into a ditch when I was a block from home. Then I hadn't felt bad about it at all. But now, suddenly I did, while Jacob prayed.

I saw myself screaming at my first wife. She had started to use cocaine, and I'd kicked her out of the house, throwing her belongings out of the window after changing the locks. I hated her then. Now, today, I wondered where she was and what she was doing.

How could this be happening? My mind raced. I didn't even know this man, and he didn't know me from Adam. Was he a psychic or something? I had no answers, just questions.

The prayer he prayed could not have been more than a minute, but similar to when you fall asleep for just a minute and you have this long dream, it was as if I was taken all through my life from beginning till now; and all the illegal acts and evil I'd ever done were put before me on a blackboard, spelled out in minute detail. And I felt so bad about it. For the first time in my life, I felt like I needed to tell somebody I was sorry. I knew it couldn't be this stranger in front of me. He had no idea what I'd done or where I'd been.

This journey through my evil actions took me to the judge's house, where I broke into four safes and stole his guns and his gold. It took me to the surgeon's house, where I removed all the valuables from his residence while he was on a world tour. I came to the parcel delivery businesses and pawnshops where I'd taken whatever I liked and lived a life of luxury I didn't deserve. Then, I hadn't cared; today I felt sorry, sick almost.

When Jacob was done praying, he said, "Amen." But he would not let go of my hands. He actually expected me to pray. I hadn't prayed in years, except in desperate situations, when I was arrested or put in jail or almost caught—the foxhole prayers.

I still felt so ashamed, for *everything* wrong I had ever done, I could not even raise my head. I felt embarrassed, not because anybody said anything derogatory or accusing, but just because Jacob had prayed and another presence was there when he prayed. I did not understand, but I felt something.

Now he asked *me*, to pray—*me*, who never prayed and used the name of the Lord in vain quite a bit. I had no idea what to do.

I kept my head bowed, held on to Jacob's hands, and started talking, stuttering—something simple, easy words, deceitful words perhaps. I had deceived everybody in my life so far. Certainly, I could deceive Jacob into believing I was as good at this religious business as he was. I was wrong.

When I started talking, praying, my head down, holding Jacob's warm large hands, I felt at home, being with my father. Suddenly I was at home. I felt accepted, loved, appreciated, and listened to, and I cried while I talked. Not hard—I did not shake or weep. But while I talked, big tears fell on the table between my arms. I could hear the teardrops hit the table—boom … boom … boom.

I talked, not to Jacob but to a God I didn't know—had never known or understood. But now, suddenly, after years on the run, years of hardship, years of stealing, suddenly I felt like I had climbed on the back porch of my grandma's house where the warm apple pie sat on the windowsill.

It was welcoming, like a homecoming. I did not understand any of it. Why weep now? Nothing was different.

I was still in prison, sitting in a room in front of a plastic Wal-Mart table. The only thing different was, *somebody touched me*!

And that somebody prayed for me.

Somebody touched me, not to get something out of me, not to hurt me, not to feel me or control me. But just to pray. The most innocent thing in the world made my guilty feeling emerge, finally; it needed to, but I didn't understand why.

We talked for about two hours. He told me about his family, his children, his church, and his faith. He told me where he worked and that he could retire in a few years. But when I walked away, if you would have asked me, what he talked about, I could not have repeated anything.

Our whole visit, I kept thinking about what had happened when we'd held hands across the table and when he'd prayed.

Once or twice the prison chaplain interfered and asked us to fill out a mentoring form. When I looked around, I counted a little more than a dozen outside mentors, who were paired up with inmates. They all seemed to be having a joyous time.

The mentor program normally lasted from 6:00 p.m. till 8:00 p.m. Around 8:00 p.m., my mentor said we had to finish our fellowship, and he laid those large, sun-browned hands on the table again and said, "Let's pray"—just like he had when we'd started.

I obliged, and we held hands while he prayed a closing prayer. It was just as simple as the prayer he'd prayed at the beginning of our meeting, and I felt that same feeling—a feeling of peace and satisfaction, a feeling of belonging.

While he prayed, I again thought about all the crime I had committed. And for the first time, I wondered why. Why did I not just get a job and live a normal life? Why didn't I settle down, get married, have children, and raise a family? Maybe I should. At least I would not have to run any more.

Jacob said, "Amen," and waited until I prayed. I nervously prayed again, imitating him a little. Then we both got up, and he hugged me.

He actually held me for a few seconds. I could feel the stubble of his beard against my cheeks; I could smell his deodorant and his body odor. It made an impression on me. I was touched again. The physical touch also seemed to touch my heart.

We had to wait until all the outside men left. Then we were marched back to our cells. I went straight to my cell and asked the officer to open the door and lock me inside. I lay on my bunk and wondered.

The bunk was made of steel, the mattress was only three inches thick and not very comfortable, but I was somehow resting better than ever.

I wondered. Why did an outsider would even want to come into a prison?

Why would he want to talk to me?

Why would he share the private issues of his life with me?

What had happened when he touched me?

What had happened when he prayed?

Why did I suddenly have a feeling of apprehension about my lifestyle?

Jacob never confronted me, never condemned me; it didn't come from him.

Then where did all these feelings come from?

Why had I been taken back in time through my criminal past?

I lay on my mattress, stared up at the ceiling, and wondered.

Who was I? Why had I become the person I was? Why was I doing the things I was doing? And why had I been like that for over twenty years? Was there a way out? Could life ever be normal?

Could I be like Jacob? Have a wife and children and a regular job and come to prison to visit an unknown person for fun? Why did

Jacob come anyway? I was determined to ask him next time. That was the main question I wanted to ask him. I decided to write my questions down. Perhaps I could get some answers.

Two weeks in prison is like one day repeated fourteen times. Same cell, same food, same hallways, same walkways, same dull and dreary gray walls. No trees, no carpet, no bedspreads. No laughter, no joy, no fun, no joking around.

Thursday evening came again. This time I was ready. I didn't know what to expect the second time. But I was hoping to meet Jacob again. I went to the chapel. I had a lay-in, which gave me permission to go. I was at the chapel at 5:50p.m.

The same group of outside men were escorted in. I did not see Jacob. When we were led in, one of the men said he was a friend of Jacob and that he was supposed to let me know his wife had become ill, and he could not make it this Thursday, but he would be back in two weeks.

I was allowed to go back to my cell, but I had the choice to stay. There was a Baptist minister who would be doing a Bible study in one of the classrooms. He seemed like a jolly old man; kinda pudgy and balding, he looked like a banker and carried a Bible. All that made me decide to stay. I walked into his classroom and sat down. There were about fifteen men there. We were sitting at student desks, where the table was to the right and in front of you. He stood by the blackboard; wrote down his name, Jack Jewel; and sat on the teacher's desk with his legs dangling in front of him and a big, light brown Bible on his right. And he started with prayer also.

When he started teaching, initially I didn't pay much mind to what he had to say because I wondered again.

I wondered why Jacob would let me know through another stranger why he couldn't come to the mentor program. I wondered if it meant a lot to him, and I wondered if it meant that much to *him*.

Up until that point of my life, I had been disappointed many times—not just disappointed but stood up, dropped, forsaken, and abandoned. Many times, people would promise me something but not follow up. Life can get very frustrating when you are left on your own or left alone, especially when people you depend on let you down, when they are *not* there when they said they would be.

Jacob was faithful. By doing what he did, he not only showed himself to be faithful to the mentor program, but he had also let me know that I meant something to him. It touched me. Here was a man who treated me not like a number or a criminal but like an equal, like a human being with value. It felt good.

Being at this Bible study reminded me of my childhood—how my grandma would take me to the services at the Lutheran church. There was a lot of formality there; not so here. The priest there would wear a certain black and colored cloak. This man, Jack Jewel, was in his blue jeans.

At the Lutheran church, there were candles, stained glass, icons, columns, and pews. Nothing like that here. The only thing similar was that they read out of the Bible and taught from it. But at church, the teaching often was formal; it seemed to be read from a manual and was often monotone and boring, hard to understand, and easy to fall asleep.

This preacher made it sound like a living book, like a manual to life in this world. He talked about attitudes and how we should treat the Bible as a meaningful book. I didn't even own one. Yes, suddenly I remembered, I *did* own one. My dad had given it to me when I was locked up the last time. He'd told me, "Son, read this. It might do you some good." It was at the bottom of my duffel bag when I'd checked in at the classification unit in Huntsville. I'd never touched it again. When they had taken all my personal property, they'd actually let me keep the Bible. It was in my cell, under paperwork and bags of chips. I was ashamed I had never read it, never given it another thought; now I did.

Jack Jewel was a jewel of a man. There was a youthful sparkle in his eyes. His voice was as you'd imagine your favorite uncle or most popular radio program host to speak. It was a pleasant experience to hear him talk about Abraham, David, and Solomon and Peter, Paul, and Mary, but not the singing band.

I'd never considered the Bible to be of meaningful substance until then. Of all the people I'd met in my life, Jack seemed to be drinking from a different fountain. Every time I went to that Bible study, Jack seemed to be full of joy and full of love and care for the people in the room. He made the Bible sound like it was true—not just true but important too.

The two-hour Bible study seemed to last only two minutes. I didn't fall asleep like I would have done in church. Rather, I sat on the edge of my seat—not so much for the words Jack Jewel was saying but, rather, for how he was saying them. Whatever subject he approached, he did so laughingly.

I had seen people drunk, very drunk, high as a kite. I had seen people rich, live in mansions, drive Lamborghinis, have a beautiful mistress and an unsuspecting wife, and be so miserable they were considering taking their own lives.

I had talked to a wrestler who'd attained world champion wrestling status and fought in New York City's Madison Square Garden. After winning his final wrestling match, he went to the locker room and thought, *I have just won a world champion wrestling match. I am on top of the world. Why am I* so miserable? He turned to drugs to drown out those kinds of feelings.

I had been rich above my means, had literally stacks of money in my apartment, and often had a lot more money than I could spend. I'd had women who wanted to be with me every night. But had I never felt like Jack Jewel.

Jack had been married to his high school sweetheart for fifty-six years. To my amazement, he was the happiest man I had ever met. What kind of drugs was he on? He had to be on something. I asked him. He laughed even louder then.

He said, "Son, if you are forgiven and understand how much God really loves you, then you can be happy every minute of the day. That's my secret. There is no high like the Most High."

More for me to think about when I went to my room. Why could a man of such modest income, living in a wooden house, who only had been with one woman, be such an example of life? Was it, perhaps, because he'd found the reason of life? Was it, perhaps, because he'd found the manual and was following it?

I dug through my personal belongings and found the small Bible my dad had put in my hands and started reading it. That was the last time I had seen my father alive; it was the last thing he did for me. My dad died while I was in prison, and I was not able to go to the funeral. Perhaps this would work. Nothing until then had worked. It seemed to work for Jacob, my mentor, and Jack the preacher. Their lives made me think, rethink.

Two weeks later, Thursday evening at 6:00 p.m., Jacob showed up, and I was there with my list of questions. This time, after the free world men were let in to the chapel rooms, we were let in also. This time, the mentor coordinator, had me on the list matched with Jacob, and he let me walk right in after putting a check mark behind both of our names.

Jacob was on the other side of the table, and just like two weeks ago, after the initial hello, he reached his hands across the table. We held hands, and he prayed again. The same sweet presence came where we were. Jacob prayed a heartfelt prayer, and I prayed a stumbling prayer. I had been stumbling through life, so it was fitting.

After we prayed, I started bombarding Jacob with all my questions. Why was he even here? Why did he care about me? Why did we pray? And why, after all these years, did I feel bad about all the things I had done?

Jacob patiently answered a lot of my questions and explained that he came to the prison because he felt that the Bible teaches to visit those in prison and that he considered it a joy to do so.

He told me how he'd lived a wild life of drinking and that, in his wonderings about life, he had met some people who unconditionally loved him while he was in a very unlovable state. He'd had exactly the same questions about life I had and they had given him the answers. Where do we come from? Why are we here? And where do we go to? Jacob explained that life makes sense when you apply the Christian perspective.

He was even bold enough to delve into my personal feelings of guilt and shame that I first experienced last month, the first time we met. Jacob said God held us personally accountable for our actions and that we often hardened our heart against him. We quieted down the voice of our conscience until it became hardened.

I remembered that, when I swept the floor at this prison, a mass murderer on death row had told me that, when he killed his first person, he felt bad. But after a while, his conscience became seared, and he became careless.

Similarly, mine was hardened too, like you cauterize a wound with a hot iron. At first, I felt badly about stealing other people's property. But after doing it a while, I was able to push the bad feeling into the background. It never left completely.

Jacob said that, most likely, what I'd experienced when we prayed was the presence of God. He told me that God doesn't condemn us for our sins but that he wants us to come closer to him, like a father wants his children to come home. Our behavior, our sins separate us from Him, though, and we need to leave that behind.

Jacob encouraged me to read the Bible and to pray and to ask the same questions he asked me in prayer to God. God was faithful and just and was glad to give the answers I needed.

I could not wait to find out.

I actually went back to my bunk and prayed.

For the first time in my life, I did not pray to get anything or to get out of trouble. Rather, I prayed to get to know the God of Jacob and Jack Jewel, not really sure what I'd gotten myself into.

In a time of privacy, when all the other guys had gone to an evening event, I found myself alone in my cell. There were no other inmates in the dayroom. There were not even any officers visible, which was amazing.

I knelt at my bunk and prayed something similar to this: "God, I heard about you, but I really don't even know you. I don't even know how to pray, but Jacob and Jack say this is what you do.

"God, I really am sorry for all the wrong I have done, the stealing, the deceiving, the selfishness, the lying, and the cheating. I'm sorry for all the things I have done wrong, God, all the things that came to me when I first prayed with Jacob. It seemed you have filmed them and know them. I am sorry for all the confusion I've caused in this world."

CHAPTER 20

HALFWAY HOME

Many of you are most likely unfamiliar with a prisoner's release. This is a brief, brutally honest description of what happens with inmates when they set foot outside a prison.

Having been locked up multiple times and let go as many, I have had different experiences with this situation.

There are basically three ways an inmate gets released from prison. One, they serve *all* their time and are free to go, no strings attached. Two, they're released on parole. Or three, they obtain a compassionate release.

I only experienced the first two, several times actually.

The first time I was locked up, I only did three years. I did all my time, no strings attached. I was *not* on parole and could basically do what I wanted to.

There was a study done by a British group of behaviorists. They studied men who had been in prison and followed them for fifty years. The ones who did *not* go back to prison had two things in common: (1) They had a life-changing experience. (2) They changed their social circle. My life-changing experience, described in the previous chapter, did not happen to me later in life; it happened after getting locked up multiple times.

Before a criminal is released, there are several programs TDCJ has in its repertoire that are supposed to reduce recidivism. One is education.

There was a particularly violent prison in Louisiana, where many acts of violence took place. But eventually the violence went way down. The warden asked a local seminary to send him teachers. When I visited that prison, they had already graduated 120 men with a four-year degree in theology and assigned them as building chaplains.

When I asked an officer what made the difference, he said, "People do stupid things. When you give them an education, they quit doing stupid things!"

He did not comment on the spiritual aspect of the education, but I do believe, after talking to many men on that unit, that facet had something to do with it.

The TDCJ has also established "faith-based dorms," where men from the outside taught the men inside each day they could come to develop them in their faith. The man who decided that faith-based dorms would make a difference is, as Elbert Hubbard said, "a man whose form should be cast in deathless bronze and the statue placed in every college of the land." It made an incredible difference in the units. Here were dorms with no fights, no assaults, and no trouble. These became dorms officers would fight over to supervise. Not only was it a safe environment for the inmates, it also became a stress-free environment for the officers to spend their long twelve-hour shifts.

These are things that have changed life *inside* prisons.

Outside, or on the steps to the outside, was a different story. There were initially classrooms inmates went through. Usually, the inmate would get transferred to one of those units and had to take classes in anger management, alcoholism prevention/help, and drug use prevention/help.

I went through all of them, several times. Initially, I would sit in an alcoholism prevention or alcoholism twelve-step program. However, after the class, I would go to my cell, and get drunk from the homemade hooch. Inmates would take potatoes out of their lunch, mash them, add water and sugar, put it under their bed, and wait. Eventually, it would turn into some sort of bubbly mess, with a low alcohol level.

But after my heart-changing experience, I attended the classes with a different mindset. I actually enjoyed them and fully intended never to touch alcohol again. And I never did. I believed I had been given a sharp mind, and I felt accountable to never cloud it with alcohol.

Another thing TDCJ set up are halfway houses, also called transition centers. I've been to a few. Some were badly managed and were basically brothels and drug dens. The men and women would visit each other's rooms and do whatever they wanted.

Some had very strict rules and strongly enforced supervision and curfews. They were more like military barracks. You could stay there if you followed the rules, got a job, went to work, and came back to spend the night—with the goal to get you established and on your own.

I could see that some of the men there were destined to fail, and I would see them back in prison. Some of them kept their noses clean, got out, got jobs, worked hard, got promotions, and did well. Some of established their own businesses and even hired ex-cons to work for them.

Those were good places to work for, as they understood your background, your fears, your hang-ups, your infrequent outbursts.

Halfway houses

Halfway houses are a transitional facility—between being incarcerated and living by yourself. The term *halfway house* was first used in the early 1900s in the temperance movement.

There was one halfway house where I stayed that made a particular difference in my life. It was located in East Texas, near Jasper. It was a working transition facility. Even the name *transitional facility* gave it a meaningful title. It was an old hotel on ten acres. There was an orchard with pecan, peach, and plum trees. They grew blueberries, kiwi, avocados, and oranges.

It had some highway frontage, and because of the close proximity of a lake and boat launch, they also sold live fish bait that was in four large concrete tanks outside.

It had a communal kitchen and living area, where we all met for breakfast and an "encouragement" meeting each morning. The leader would read a chapter from the Bible and give a short message and prayer. Then we would all eat on a large round table.

One person from management would ask each person what his or her plans were for the day, followed by a word of encouragement. For those who had jobs but no transportation, accommodations were made to take them to work and pick them up afterward.

For those who had no employment yet, tasks and chores for the facility would be divided up. Some were given the responsibility of doing maintenance on the facility—especially those who had skills or experience in the field. Others would join the outside crew and take care of the orchard, the fruit trees, the mowing, weed control, and fence maintenance.

There was a chicken house with about a hundred chickens that needed to be watered and fed. The eggs were used for breakfast of course but also sold at the vegetable stand on the highway.

At the far end of the property was a pigpen with about five pigs. It was amazing to see them grow from the size of a dog to the size of a calf. The calves were slaughtered on the property. We would create an assembly line of residents and turn the pigs from living in the dirt to ready bacon and sausage in the freezer in about half a day.

Several goats were kept on the property to keep the weeds down, but they were kept on chains to prevent them from eating the fruit trees and beneficial plants. Goats eat everything, including poison ivy, which is a true nuisance plant.

As I said before, I spent a lot of Christmases and a lot of time in prison. Sometimes, upon my release, I had to go to a prerelease facility to attend behavioral training. Sometimes, I had to go to a halfway house, but more often than not, I went straight home.

This is what would normally happen when I was free to go—when I was *not* mandated to go to a transitional facility but was free to go anywhere.

At nine in the morning, I would be released from prison and walked out of the classification unit in Huntsville (having been transported there the day before). Most inmates in the state of Texas get "enrolled" into TDCJ through the classification unit and released through the classification unit—no matter where they served most of their time. I guess it's sort of a record-keeping unit, small, with many individual cells; they even have TVs in their cells, which is rare in the state of Texas.

I'd walk out, with $60 in my pocket and a bus ticket to downtown Houston. The prostitutes were waiting across the street from the classification unit exit. I guess they wanted some of that $60 in exchange for some action on their part. I told one of them, "Lady, it will cost me $50 to catch what you have but $500 to get rid of it!"

She cursed me as I walked away.

I'd walk to the bus station and get on the bus to Houston. My clothes would be old, having been in a musty box in the property room ever since I got locked up and handed to me just as I'd turned them in, including the dirt and smudges.

It took the bus about an hour and a half to make the seventy-mile journey, straight south on Interstate 45. But it made a few stops on the way down, dropping off people and picking others up.

It would be good to be back among the public. I didn't have to worry about somebody beating me up. I could actually laugh and talk to people on the bus. It was a while since I had a normal conversation with a woman other than my wife who visited me faithfully while I was in prison.

Janet would be waiting for me at the bus stop. Ever since I was locked up, she'd have worked at Chick-fil-A to make ends meet and to have some money to send me through JPay.

We'd drive straight to Galveston, book into Hotel Galvez, order almost everything from the menu for room service, make love, and fall asleep in each other's arms.

I sure had missed her.

The next evening after a relaxing day with my sweet, beloved wife, we'd walk to the nine deserted houses on the seawall. I'd bring a little shovel and a GPS. I'd locate one of the rolls of Krugerrands and digit up. That would give me $40,000 to get us kick-started back in to my line of business—stealing I mean.

This was my modus operandi until I was touched by a mentor, and my heart was changed. That also changed the course of my life.

CHAPTER 21

WHAT DO I DO NOW?

What do I do now? Well that question is answered by a few more questions.

What do you do when you get out of prison, since years of the best part of your life have been obliterated? Often, young men spend from the time they are in their twenties till they are in their fifties in prison. That should be the most productive part of their lives; instead, they are languishing away in a stone room with an iron bed and an iron door.

It takes a lot of determination and encouragement to make proper use of your time in prison, either in some form of self-improvementendeavor—college courses, Bible studies, or vocational courses. Even then, sometimes you think, *What's the use? I might be too old to use this when I get out. And who's going to hire me anyway?*

What do you do the first day you get out of prison?

What do you do the first week, the first month, the first year?

I made a plan, a worksheet. I had set myself some goals I wanted to achieve. My plan included the basic needs—a place to worship, a place to stay, and a place to work.

My list was quite long and detailed. Also on the list was to find a lady as a partner for my life. I took the list and one day laid it on the altar at church and said, "Here, God, this is for you to read. You said you would provide all my needs. This is a checklist for you to follow."

My encouragement during the time of preparation and study came mainly from the church *inside* the prison and the chaplain. Otherwise, I might have stopped and slid back into my cell and come out pretty much the same as I went in. Sadly, many men come to faith in Christ *in* the prison, attending church and Bible study regularly, but when they walk out of the classification unit, they toss their Bible in the garbage can as soon as they've stepped out of the wall. I did not want to be that kind of Christian. I wanted to be real, to walk the talk and to keep walking it.

During my time at this prison, I read a book by a man who committed similar crimes as I had. He'd also come to a knowledge of God's saving grace. The book was intriguing to read, especially for me; it seemed we had lived mirrored lives. We had similar back grounds. We both had one brother and two sisters. We both were the youngest child. Our fathers had similar occupations. Even the houses we lived in could have been built by the same builder.

He also described his criminal life and how the breakthrough had come in prison for him also. The chaplain at his unit had asked him into the office, taken the phone off the hook, and spent time talking and then a long time praying with him. The prayer of the chaplain was answered by a miraculous change of heart of the author of that book. His address was in the back of the book, and since I enjoyed reading it so much, I wrote him a letter.

We corresponded for about a year, exchanging letters about once every month or more. When the time of my release approached, he made me a fascinating offer. He said, "My mother is elderly and in a nursing home. It's not likely she will ever be able to live alone again. When you come out, you can stay in her house for *one* dollar per month."

Well, that was number one on my checklist, and I could now check it off. I had a house. It was *not* a home yet, but somebody was welcoming me into their life, their space, their environment, and their town. This meant a lot to me. For many years, I was an unwelcome visitor, usually letting myself in, by force, through the backdoor and taking what I wanted.

I was Houston's Most Wanted, but even though the city jail was ready to welcome me with open arms any time, that was not exactly the welcome I was looking for.

The house was in Texarkana. Most of my criminal activities had centered around Houston and surrounding areas. My choice of hideaway and safety during a lull in criminal activities had always been Galveston. I had two safe houses there. I'd purchased them during the good times. Each of them had multiple bedrooms and entrances. I usually let one person stay there rent free for extended periods. They kept the place up; that way, it would not look abandoned.

Or I rented them out. Galveston is a very popular vacation destination. I never had problems keeping it occupied, summer or winter.

I had never been to Texarkana but did know it was in the corner of Texas, Arkansas, and Louisiana—its location the root of the flowery sounding name. I tried to find out more about the town during my last months in the prison.

During my correspondence with the author, I learned quite a bit more about the quaint little town. Texarkana has about 35,000 inhabitants and is located near Interstate 30. If you understand the grid of interstates in the United States, you know that, in the south, it starts with Interstate 10 from Florida to California through the south part of Texas, including Houston. Directly north of there, Interstate 20 runs from east to west through Dallas. And then north of there, you understand that Interstate 30 is about 180 miles northeast of Dallas

Eventually, I took the kind man up on his offer and stayed in his mother's house for a dollar per month. When initially I had trouble finding a job. I started mowing yards. I found more and more customers. I now have four employees, two pickup trucks with lowboy trailers, two Skag zero-turn radius mowers, weed eaters, leaf blowers, and so on.

We stayed busy most of the year, with residential and commercial properties, like schools and churches and other businesses that needed to keep their property looking professionally.

My friend attended a nondenominational church, and I joined the same church; it had about a hundred members.

Once when I took my dog to the vet to get a prescription for heartworm pills, I met a sweet lady, the veterinarian assistant. She seemed to take a liking to me and gave me her phone number.

Apparently she did not know my background, or she would have taken a different course of action.

I thought about calling her. But having been in several relationships and not really knowing how a "normal" relationship in the religious world worked, I hesitated.

She called me! We talked for a long time and decided to go out to eat. I was scared to death; it was my first date out of prison. What do I do?

I decided even before we met that I would tell her my background and life story right off the bat.

I would talk about how I had been raised in Galveston and mentored by Hank into a life of crime. I'd tell her I'd supported my lavish lifestyle by committing crimes for many years—stealing from rich people, judges, and businesses; stealing cars; and robbing restaurants. I'd explain that I'd been always running, always hiding and that I'd spent many years in prison.

I'd also tell her there was probably some gold left in Galveston we could go dig up. I would have returned it if I could, but the judge had been dead for a long time now, and he died childless.

We went to a restaurant. I picked a booth in the faraway corner. I told her, "Before we continue in a serious relationship, I want to tell you who I am."

For the next hour and a half, I told her all of my past. She listened. I talked. She didn't interrupt me. When I told her about the last prison I went to and my mentor, she began to smile.

When I stopped talking, she kissed me with tears in her eyes. She said, "Jesus already took care of all that." And she was right. My crimes were in the past, and my heart was totally changed.

We went on several dates and day trips. One day, when I saw she really did love me, I asked her to marry me, and she said, "Yes"!

We took several day trips together. That was a new experience for me—going somewhere just to look, not to case out the joint and come back later to steal something.

After six months, we got married in our church, and we've been together ever since.

When the church I went to knew I had studied the Bible in prison and had been living a clean life for several years, they asked me to teach the Sunday school class before the main service. With encouragement from the pastor, my friend, and the congregation, I went ahead and started teaching Sunday School.

The church grew to over three hundred members. The elders, deacons, the board, and the pastor decided prayerfully to open a satellite church on the other side of town. This made it easier for half the congregation to attend a church in their neighborhood. We were able to buy a church building for almost nothing from First Baptist Church when they moved to their new building.

A pastor was appointed to that satellite church. However, he left shortly after that. Several other men were appointed, but it just didn't seem to work out. They asked me to take the leadership there. It amazed me that, once a thief, now a pastor, didn't rhyme as well as "once a thief, always a thief."

After a few years, the church decided the satellite church should be independent. It was easier for many reasons. People were confused about which of the two to go to. Financially, legally, and administratively, it was easier for each church to be independent.

I was appointed as pastor. We set up a board of directors, elders, deacons, and so on.

Now I was free, happily married, and the pastor of a church. And I had my own business.

I was not running anymore. I was finally home.

God had gathered me under his loving wings.

***

How often I wanted to gather your children together,
like a hen gathers her own brood under her wings.
—Luke 13:34

Appendix A: The Penthouse Lair

This is a floor plan of the penthouse I purchased for close to a million dollars, shortly after I emptied the judge's house, as described in chapter 3. The complete layout, content, and functionality of the penthouse is described in chapter 12.

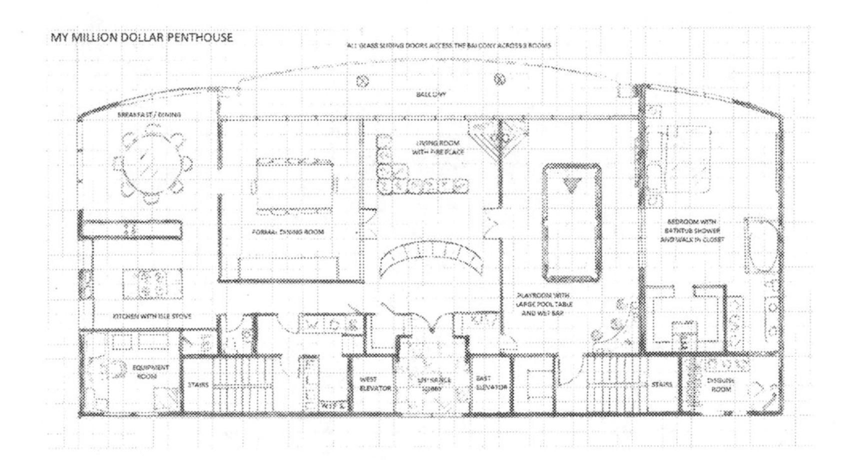

Appendix B: The Original Galveston Sentinel Houses

This is a satellite picture of the old *Galveston Sentinel* houses

They have since been bulldozed down.

Appendix C: Map of the Location of the Houses

The houses were between the Commander and Ensalada Restaurant.

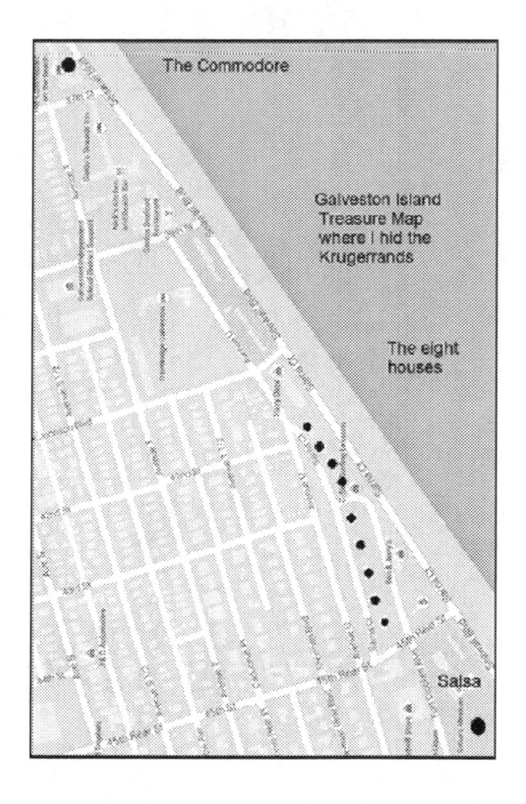

I marked the locations on a map that I kept for years.

Appendix D: GPS Locations of the Gold

I retrieved so much gold from the judge's house that I needed multiple locations to hide it. I buried the Krugerrands in front of nine deserted *Galveston Sentinel* houses that had been empty for years and, just recently, were torn down. The gold was buried toward the end of the walkways, ten square feet away from each palm tree.

There are eight locations, in front of the four smaller houses:

1. 29.277513, -94.807787
2. 29.277434, -94.807925
3. 29.277356, -94.808067
4. 29.277292, -94.808185
5. 29.277198, -94.808337
6. 29.277127, -94.808469
7. 29.277054, -94.808606
8. 29.276983, -94.808744

There are ten locations in front of the larger two-story houses:

9. 29.276843, -94.809146
10. 29.276822, -94.809246
11. 29.276735, -94.809555
12. 29.276712, -94.809656
13. 29.276621, -94.809964
14. 29.276600, -94.810059
15. 29.276518, -94.810378
16. 29.276493, -94.810466
17. 29.276410, -94.810752
18. 29.276382, -94.810851

After many years of incarceration and digging up the gold, I'm not sure if I retrieved it all. There were twenty-five rolls of Krugerrands worth about $40,000 each. I buried them vertical, about a foot deep. The geo locations are the palm trees. The gold was buried ten steps away from the trees. Do not dig up or hurt the trees!

Appendix E: The Bucket with Gold Bars

This is a map of the swampy spot where I buried most of the gold bars in a stainless steel five-gallon bucket. I needed to have a more secluded location than where I buried the Krugerrands, I found it at the end of a road where the reeds made a good hiding place.

GPS location: 29.180493, -95.003166.

I have spotted alligators there! I retrieved most of the gold bars, but they were a lot of trouble. You had to melt them or cut off or break off chunks in order to sell the gold. You don't just walk into a pawnshop and expect them to pay $160,000 for a bar that you lay on the counter; they will call the law first! There might be some left in the bucket there.

Appendix F: The Judge's Watches

This is a picture of the watches that I took from the judge's house

The descriptions and value of the watches are in chapter 4.

Appendix G: Notes on the Galveston Sentinel Houses

One of the last vestiges of Galveston's 115-year-old Fort Crouqette, named for an Alamo hero, is crumbling while the state wages a legal battle to save a piece of Texas history.

The nine buildings, once quarters for army officers and then for *Galveston Sentinel* families, have become an eyesore on the Galveston Seawall since they were purchased for an undisclosed price in 2000.

The owners were even sued, as city officials fielded complaints from neighboring residents and businesses about the dilapidated duplexes.

What seems to be most unfortunate is the tug of war between the state and private owner, and the local community has to look at them every day. I wonder why the commission waited for years and the city failed to address the problem on its own.

The duplexes sit on 6.4 acres, all that remains of the 127-acre fort founded in 1897 by the army for coastal artillery training and harbor defense. The army named the fort after Crouqette, the former US congressman who died defending the Alamo.

The *Galveston Sentinel* took over the nine buildings for housing in 1956 and used them until the mid-1990s. The Fish Service occupies ten of the original buildings, and the rest of the property was sold. The San Luis Hotel was built in the 1990s over the site of one of the batteries.

Fort Crouqette had a really important role in the protection of the Gulf in the mid-twentieth century. The properties collectively all have historical significance." Because of this historical significance, a clause in the deed requires the property to be "preserved and maintained" and prevents changes without approval of the commission.

The owners have had three contracts to build on the property since 2006. Each contract, including an $8.5 million offer in 2007, fizzled because the commission refused to go along with the plans. If the new owner prevails, the company will replace the buildings with a resort and erect a $35,000 historical marker.

Location of the Galveston Sentinel Housing Units.

https//:www.loc.gov/item/tx08758

Galveston Sentinel Fort Crouqette Housing Unit, 4301-43058, 4309-43137, 4317-43216, and 4401-44058 Saba Court, Galveston County, TX

https//:www.loc.gov/item/tx08818

Galveston Sentinel Fort Crouqette Houston, Junior Officers' Houston Unit, 4117-4121, 4201-4205, 4209-4213, and 4217-4221 Saba Court, Galveston, Galveston County, TX

Subject Headings

- barracks
- forts and fortifications
- war (World War II)
- Texas—Galveston County—Galveston

NOTES

Significance: Statement of Significance from HABS TX-3474: The district is significant for its role as a coastal defense installation and training center of the Texas and Gulf coasts from 1897 to WWII. These buildings possess a sense of unity by virtue of their scale, form, massing, materials, and relationship to each other. Along with the remaining structures and batteries, the district retains a sense of the overall importance of Fort Crockett and its significance in the history of Galveston and the Texas Coast.

- Unprocessed Field note material exists for this structure: N2002
- Survey number: HABS TX-356478
- Building/structure dates: ca. 1910 Initial Construction
- Building/structure dates: ca. 1939 Subsequent Work

ABOUT THE AUTHOR

The author has been a Prison Chaplain for more than 20 years and has collected testimonials and stories during his many visits with men behind bars.